W9-CKM-521

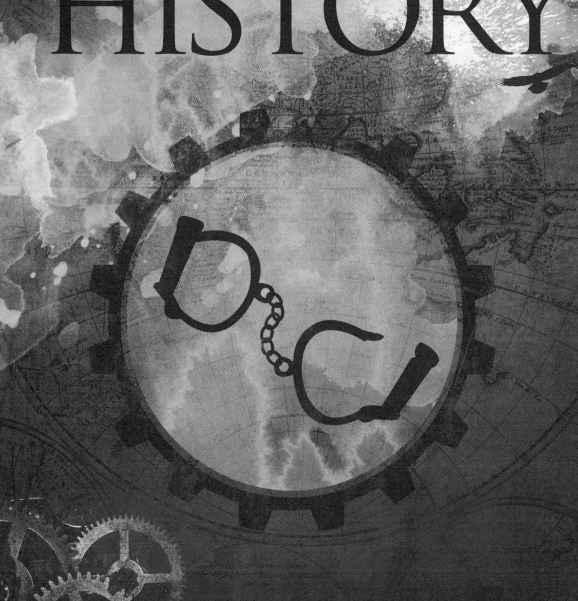

# TWISTED
# HISTORY

## METRO BOOKS

### New York

METRO BOOKS and the distinctive Metro Books logo are trademarks
of Sterling Publishing Co., Inc.

© 2015 Quantum Books Ltd

All rights reserved. No part of this publication may be reproduced,
stored in a retrieval system or transmitted in any form or by any means
(including electronic, mechanical, photocopying, recording, or otherwise)
without prior written permission from the publisher.

This book was designed, conceived, and produced by
Quantum Books Ltd
6 Blundell Street
London N7 9BH
United Kingdom

Publisher: Kerry Enzor
Quantum Editorial: Sam Kennedy and Hazel Eriksson
Production Manager: Rohana Yusof
Design: Amazing 15

ISBN 978-1-4351-5785-9
For information about custom editions, special sales, and premium
and corporate purchases, please contact Sterling Special Sales at
800-805-5489 or specialsales@sterlingpublishing.com.

Manufactured in China by 1010 Printing International Ltd.

2 4 6 8 10 9 7 5 3 1

www.sterlingpublishing.com

# TWISTED HISTORY

32 True Stories of Torture,
Traitors, Sadists, and Psychos...
plus the most celebrated saints in history

## HOWARD WATSON

METRO BOOKS
New York

# Contents

## TREACHERY & TORTURE

# SAINTS & SINNERS

# MURDER & MAYHEM

# Introduction

From the beginning of human existence there has been a darkness that has accompanied almost all the major events in the world: the tales are stained with murder, assassination, torture, betrayal, lust, revenge, remorselessness, and boundless ambition. The darkness is not unique to narratives of serial killers, gangsters, torturers, and assassins, and their sometimes almost unspeakable depravity. Close examination of the life of almost every king or queen, emperor, politician, and even priests and saints, reveals its own twisted history.

Different characteristics of twisted history are borne out in the three sections of this book—Treachery & Torture, Saints & Sinners, and Murder & Mayhem—although each of the themes bleeds, quite literally, into the others.

## TRAITORS—IN A CAUSE?

Treachery & Torture focuses on those who have shaken free of the constraints of honor and humanity, and embraced the dark side. Brutus, Guy Fawkes, Benedict Arnold, and Pierre Laval are all marked as the greatest of traitors against each of their own states, deviously plotting against the lives of their fellow countrymen or leaders. And yet there is often light and shade within the twists of their connivance: Brutus and Fawkes turned to assassination to uphold their own beliefs; Laval, the French prime minister who collaborated with the Nazis, believed, until his dying breath, that he was helping his own country; and Arnold . . . well, he betrayed America because of injured pride and financial gain, but even he had previously fought with valor and risked his life for his country.

Then there are those whose actions are darker still: the men implicated in mass torture and who seemed to revel in the gore, such as Adolf Eichmann, the cold-hearted architect of the Holocaust; Lavrentiy Beria, Stalin's diabolical henchman; and Gilles de Rais, the mass murderer of children. The dark depravity of some of the instruments of torture and execution is highlighted: the rack, the strappado, and, perhaps the most nausea-inducing form of execution, being hanged, drawn, and quartered. This method of dispatch, sanctioned by the English state as the punishment for treason, deliberately kept victims alive as long as possible so they could witness their own emasculation and disembowelment.

Saints & Sinners explores the lives both of those who

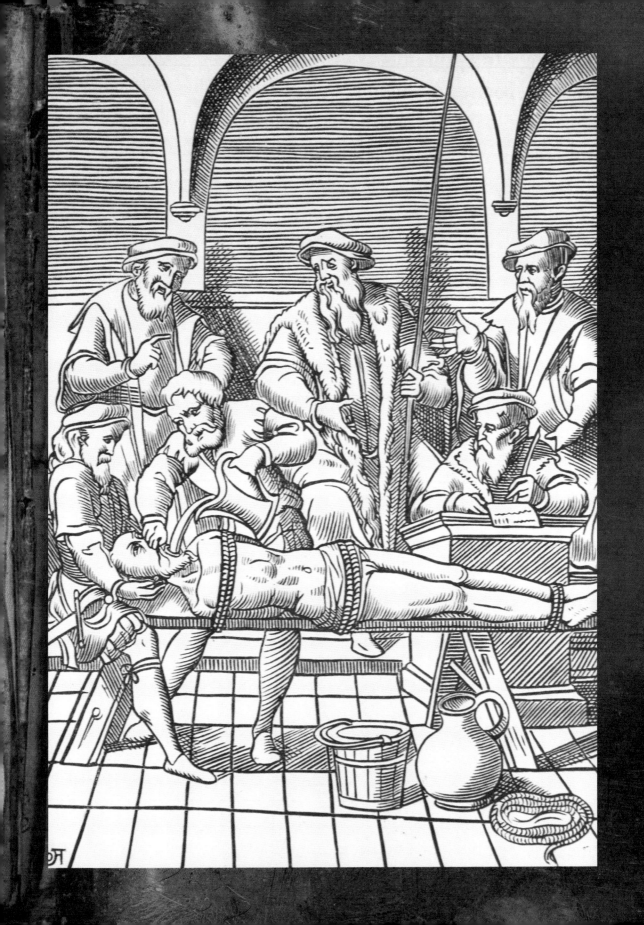

## V. R.
# £8000 REWARD
### ROBBERY and MURDER.

**W**HEREAS EDWARD KELLY, DANIEL KELLY, STEPHEN HART and JOSEPH BYRNE have been declared OUTLAWS in the Colony of Victoria, and whereas warrants have been issued charging the aforesaid men with the WILFUL MURDER of MICHAEL SCANLON, Police Constable of the Colony of VICTORIA, and whereas the above-named offenders are STILL at LARGE and have recently committed divers felonies in the Colony of NEW SOUTH WALES; Now, therefore, I, SIR HERCULES GEORGE ROBERT ROBINSON, the GOVERNOR &c. by this, my proclamation issued with the advice of the Executive Council, hereby notify that a REWARD of £4,000 will be paid, three-fourths by the Government of NEW SOUTH WALES, and one-fourth by certain Banks trading in the Colony, for the apprehension of the above-named Four Offenders, or a reward of £1000 for the apprehension of any one of them, and that in ADDITION to the above reward, a similar REWARD of £4000 has been offered by the Government of VICTORIA, and I further notify that the said REWARD will be equitably apportioned between any persons giving information which shall lead to the apprehension of the offenders and any members of the police force or other persons who may actually effect such apprehension or assist thereat.

(Signed) HENRY PARKES,
Colonial Secretary, New South Wales

(Signed) BRYAN O'LOGHLEN,
Attorney General, Victoria

Dated 15th February, 1879.

# GHASTLY
# MURDER
## IN THE EAST-END.
### DREADFUL MUTILATION OF A WOMAN.
## Capture : Leather Apron

Another murder of a character even more diabolical than that perpetrated in Back's Row, on Friday week, was discovered in the same neighbourhood, on Saturday morning. At about six o'clock a woman was found lying in a back yard at the foot of a passage leading to a lodging house in a Old Brown's Lane, Spitalfields. The house is occupied by a Mrs. Richardson, who lets it out to lodgers, and the door which admits to this passage, at the foot of which lies the yard where the body was found, is always open for the convenience of lodgers. A lodger named Davis was going down to work at the time mentioned and found the woman lying on her back close to the flight of steps leading into the yard. Her throat was cut in a frightful manner. The woman's body had been completely ripped open and the heart and other organs laying about the place, and portions of the entrails round the victim's neck. An excited crowd gathered in front of Mrs. Richardson's house and also round the mortuary in old Montague Street, whither the body was quickly conveyed. As the body lies in the rough coffin in which it has been placed in the mortuary the same coffin in which the unfortunate Mrs. Nicholls was first placed it presents a fearful sight. The body is that of a woman about 45 years of age. The height is exactly five feet. The complexion is fair, with wavy brown hair; the eyes are blue, and two lower teeth have been knocked out. The nose is rather large and prominent.

**Above (top):** £8,000 reward notice for the capture of Australian outlaws, the Ned Kelly gang, February 15, 1879; **Above (bottom):** Newspaper detailing the latest developments in the Jack the Ripper case, September 1888.
**Opposite:** Engraving showing Christians being punished by flogging, from a nineteenth-century Bible
**Previous page:** Illustration of water torture from a sixteenth-century woodcut.

were more sinned against than sinning, and those who just concentrated on the sinning. Martyrs, ranging from tormented religious saints to leading twentieth-century figures who were slain for promoting peace and justice, rub shoulders with those who mercilessly pursued religious persecution: Emperor Nero, who torched Christians to illuminate his garden; Torquemada, who victimized Jews; and Hitler, who carried persecution into a new realm of darkness—all revealed the darkest shade of the degeneracy of which humans are capable.

## MURDERERS, GANGSTERS, ASSASSINS

Nothing strikes fear into a population more than the threat of a serial killer, who cunningly defies the law to strike again and again, making us all too aware of the fragile and perilous nature of our existence. Murder & Mayhem uncovers the lives and modus operandi of the killers who snatched the innocent, dragged them into a world of pain, and extinguished them, only to evade capture and set off in pursuit of a fresh victim. Like serial killers, gangsters such as Al Capone have the power to cause mayhem by terrorizing the world with lawlessness, striking at the heart of both the individual and society's desperate need for security. Presidential assassins John Wilkes Booth and Lee Harvey Oswald also rent fissures in the foundations of civilization by snuffing out the lives of two much heralded and heroic American heads of state.

## UNRELIABLE NARRATORS

History is twisted and fortunes are changed by the remorseless characters, driven by greed, evil, or insanity, who transgress the boundaries of humanity, but the telling of history itself is sometimes twisted, too. As we assess the dark reputations and crimes of the historical players, we must always remember that history is written by the victors,

an idea extemporized by French historian and philosopher Michel Foucault and many others to the point that it has become a truism of historiography (the writing of history). Historians have their own dark reasons for contorting the tales of previous leaders to make them appear as monsters. Richard III, often regarded as the most treacherous and evil king of England, is to some extent the victim of historians' desire for grace and favor from his royal successors. His crown was taken by force by the Tudors, who only had a weak claim on the throne; contemporary historians became the agents of Tudor lies, blackening Richard's name in order to make the new dynasty seem less tyrannical and more valorous. To some extent, the reputations of Nero and Vlad the Impaler suffered in a similar manner.

Facts are also the victims of exaggeration and salaciousness on the part of chroniclers and historians. It is not enough that the serial killer Thug Behram killed well over a hundred people: he is associated with the deaths of 928, so the latter figure is often misused as the total number of his personal victims. History is also twisted with regard to H.H. Holmes; apparently the twenty-seven murders to which he confessed are not enough, and he is sometimes said to have killed 200 despite the absence of any evidence for such a huge figure.

There is a natural human thrill taken in reading of debauchery and vice. Perhaps more than any other historian, the Roman Suetonius played on this and reveled in the salacious, fleshing out the skeletal facts about emperors such as Caligula and Nero with a weight of conjectural claims about the sheer depths of their vice. Suetonius was always willing to conjure more darkness, to add a new, terrible twist to history. But even within the exaggeration, there is almost always the kernel of truth.

History, as these pages reveal, is twisted, dark, and soaked in blood.

# TREACHERY & TORTURE

# Brutus

## ONE OF THE MOST FAMOUS TRAITORS IN HISTORY, WHO MURDERED HIS FRIEND AND ALLY JULIUS CAESAR

*Et tu, Brute?* Julius Caesar, the dictator of Rome, uttered his final words, which became symbolic of the great betrayal of a close ally. Caesar had already successfully defended himself from the first strike, catching the arm of his enemy Casca as he thrust a dagger toward his neck. Then, with shock and surprise, he saw his friend, Brutus, among the group of assassins. "And you, too, Brutus?" he said with sorrow. He now knew that death was certain and covered his face with his toga. Brutus lunged with his own dagger, and his fellow conspirators followed suit. Caesar, blood pouring into his eyes from cuts to his head, tried to walk away but fell to the floor. The assassins gathered around his prone body and continued to stab long after he was motionless. There were twenty-three stab wounds to his body.

**Opposite:** The assassination of Julius Caesar on March 15, 44 BC, depicted by Vincenzo Camuccini in 1798.

## ∽ FACT FILE ∾

**Born:** June, 85 BC, Rome.
**Died:** October 23, 42 BC, Philippi.
**Historic Feat:** Murdered the dictator Julius Caesar and attempted to restore the Roman Republic.
**Circumstances of Death:** Committed suicide after being defeated in battle.
**Legacy:** Known for the betrayal of his close friend, Julius Caesar.

Marcus Junius Brutus, who enacted one of the most famous betrayals in history, was born in 85 BC in Rome, capital of the Roman republic. He was born into a turbulent era of political and martial machinations, and according to the Greek historian and biographer Plutarch, his own father's death involved a betrayal in 77 BC. Marcus Junius Brutus the Elder had been involved in attempts to start a civil war, but surrendered when faced with the army of Pompey the Great: "For Brutus, whether he himself betrayed his army, or whether his army changed sides and betrayed him, put himself in the hands of Pompey ... after a single day had passed, he was slain by Geminius, who was sent by Pompey to do the deed." However, some sources claim that Brutus's real father was Julius Caesar—even though Julius was only 14 years old when Brutus was conceived—in an attempt to explain their relationship.

As a young man Brutus assisted

his mother's half-brother, Cato the Younger, an acclaimed orator, and earned a fortune from moneylending while abroad in Cyprus and Cilicia. He married Claudia Pulchra on his return to Rome and became active in politics. Initially he was opposed to the aspiring, already powerful Julius Caesar, and, following his uncle Cato's lead, supported the more conservative pro-republic faction, the Optimates, in the Senate. Even though the Optimate leader, Pompey, was responsible for the death of his father, Brutus supported him in a civil war with

Caesar, which began in 49 BC, after it became increasingly clear that Caesar wished to destroy the republic in favor of autocratic rule.

In the decisive battle of the campaign, at Pharsalus in August 48 BC, Caesar instructed that Brutus should not be harmed, supporting the theory that Caesar believed himself to be Brutus's father. The battle was a disaster for the Optimates and effectively resulted in the death of the republic. Pompey fled and was assassinated in Egypt, but Caesar showed mercy to some of his adversaries, not least Brutus, who apologized for his previous actions. Caesar appointed Brutus as governor of Gaul and the young man became part of Caesar's close circle, despite the continuing enmity of his uncle Cato.

Brutus became embroiled in a minor scandal in 45 BC,

when he decided to divorce Claudia Pulchra and marry his first cousin, Porcia Catonis, Cato's daughter. Divorce in Rome was a simple and commonplace procedure in which the husband had to state his grievance against his wife, but Brutus provided none.

Brutus's affection for Cato and the republicans was greater than his loyalty to Caesar, who had effectively become his personal political sponsor, selecting Brutus to become a praetor (a kind of magistrate) for 44 BC. After the death of Pompey, Caesar took an army to Africa to mop up the lees of armed opposition and defeated Cato in 46 BC. Brutus's uncle, known for his political and moral integrity, took his own life after the defeat. Caesar then had himself appointed as the dictator of Rome, initially for ten years, and then for life.

## OPPOSING CAESAR'S DICTATORSHIP

Brutus was now willing to turn his back on the favor and privilege he had been granted by Caesar, and once again support his more altruistic principles. He joined a conspiracy of up to sixty senators, who decided to assassinate Caesar as he entered the Senate House on the Ides (15th) of March. Unwilling to shirk responsibility, and perhaps wanting to be hailed as one of the band of men who actually performed the deed, Brutus stood amongst the assassins waiting to stab the dictator to death.

After Caesar's anguished last words, the onslaught was so ferocious and chaotic that the assassins slashed their own colleagues, with Brutus incurring wounds to his hand and legs. (We have no evidence that Caesar actually said *Et tu, Brute?*, and the words are famous because English playwright William Shakespeare ascribed them to the murdered dictator in his play of 1599, *Julius Caesar*.) Plutarch claims that while Caesar lay still in a pool of blood, Brutus attempted to speak but the other assassins fled the scene. According to legend, Brutus said, *Sic semper tyrannis* ("Thus always to tyrants"), words John Wilkes Booth would repeat after assassinating US President Abraham Lincoln on April 14, 1865.

The assassins thought that the republic would be restored, but soon discovered that the populace were more devoted to the deceased dictator than democracy: to the people, Brutus was no more than a traitor. Brutus was forced to flee and spent two years in exile in Crete. In 42 BC, he attempted to defeat Caesar's adopted son, Octavian, at the Battle of Philippi in Greece, but ultimately failed and, just like his uncle Cato, committed suicide. The republic withered and Rome was ruled by emperors for more than 400 years. ✿

# IMPERIAL ASSASSINATIONS

**AUGUSTUS**, the first emperor of Rome, may well have suffered a fate similar to his adoptive father, Julius Caesar, and been assassinated. Rather than the perpetrator being his political ally, it may have been his own wife, Livia, who is suspected of administering poison in AD 14. However, as the emperor was 75, he may have died of natural causes, which would prove to be a rare event amongst his imperial successors. In the first century of the Roman Empire, Caligula, Galba, and Vitellius were all assassinated, Nero killed himself while facing certain death, and there are suspicions about the demise of Tiberius and Claudius.

# William Wallace

## THE HERO OF SCOTTISH INDEPENDENCE WHO WAS HANGED, DRAWN, AND QUARTERED FOR HIGH TREASON IN 1305

William Wallace would suffer one of the most horrific and degrading public executions in British history. The English were determined to ensure that the death of the so-called traitor would send an enduring message to all other would-be heroes of Scottish independence. On August 23, 1305, following his show-trial for treason against the king of England, Wallace was strapped naked to a wooden hurdle and assaulted by the public as he was dragged through the streets of London to Smithfield. There, he was hanged from a gallows in front of the gleeful crowds. While still conscious, he was cut down, had his genitals sliced off, and was forced to watch his own entrails being pulled from his body and burned. Only then did the killer blow come: he was decapitated and his body was cut into quarters.

His severed head was dipped in tar and displayed on a spike at London Bridge, while the four sections of his corpse were sent north, toward the rebellious Scots, and displayed in Perth, Stirling, Berwick, and Newcastle. All this only succeeded in making Wallace the greatest martyr of Scottish independence and a prized icon of resistance for centuries to come.

Wallace was not the most obvious candidate to become the greatest enemy of Edward I of England, who was laying claim to the throne of Scotland. The Scottish warrior was certainly not seeking the crown himself, but nevertheless decided to stand in Edward's path. His early life is not well documented but he was probably born in Elderslie in Renfrewshire in the 1270s, and his parents were lesser nobles. Wallace's surname means "Welshman" or more generally "foreigner," and it is possible that his ancestors only arrived in Scotland little more than a century before his

**Opposite:** Often outnumbered, the Scots fought bravely against the English army of Edward I.

## ❧ FACT FILE ❧

**Born:** 1270s, Elderslie.
**Died:** August 23, 1305, London.
**Historic Feat:** Led the Scottish resistance to English invasion.
**Circumstances of Death:** Hanged, drawn, and quartered as a traitor.
**Legacy:** The enduring hero of Scottish independence from England.

birth. It seems likely that William was a well-educated and intelligent young man, but he remained unknown to history until he suddenly burst onto the scene in 1297. From that moment on, he would never be forgotten.

Edward I had taken advantage of a crisis in the succession to the Scottish crown following the death of Alexander III of Scotland in 1286. Several different claimants emerged and civil war threatened, so the

**Above:** A Victorian depiction of the Battle of Stirling Bridge, 1297. According to a contemporary chronicle, the victorious William Wallace made a belt from the flayed skin of the despised English nobleman Hugh de Cressingham.
**Opposite:** J.R. Skelton's depiction of William Wallace being warned of an English plot to capture him in Ayr.

Scottish nobility called upon the English king to provide independent arbitration. In return, Edward demanded the lords' acknowledgment that he was the feudal overlord of Scotland. In 1292, John Balliol was made king by the Scottish lords as it had become clear that he had the strongest legal claim. However, all along Edward was eyeing the prize for himself. He bullied John and treated Scotland as little more than a vassal state.

In 1296, the Scottish lords agreed a treaty with Edward's enemy, France, leading the English king to attack the Scots at Dunbar. John was forced to abdicate and was imprisoned in the Tower of London, while Edward assumed control of the kingdom. In May 1297, William Wallace seemingly appeared out of nowhere to lead the Scottish resistance. Reputedly a huge man, he may have gained military experience fighting for Edward's armies in France. Whatever his experience, he soon proved to be a capable foe.

Wallace organized an assault on the court of Lanark and killed its English sheriff, William Heselrig. According to the fifteenth-century poem, *The Actes and Deidis of the Illustre and Vallyeant Campioun Schir William Wallace* by Blind Harry, which helped to create the legend of Wallace in Scottish folklore, the Scotsman acted in revenge for the murder of his wife by Heselrig. There is no evidence for this and it seems more likely that Wallace was spurred on by a wave of minor anti-English rebellions that were starting to take place across Scotland, including those initiated by the nobleman Andrew Moray.

## TRIUMPH AT STIRLING BRIDGE

After further individual successes, Wallace and Moray joined forces in the name of King John. Their combined impact was immediate. On September 11, 1297, they met the English army at Stirling Bridge with a force of 2,300 men. The English, led by the Earl of Surrey and Hugh de Cressingham, had an enormous numerical advantage, with up to 10,000 infantry and 2,000 cavalry, but little tactical sense. They attempted to cross a narrow bridge, thereby negating their superiority, and suffered remarkable losses. Exemplary tactics from Wallace, Moray, and their men led to the slaying of at least 5,000 English soldiers; Scottish losses may have amounted to mere hundreds.

The Scots had abandoned the prevalent mode of chivalric, fair combat to use the terrain to their advantage, giving a lesson to English generals of the future. Cressingham was killed and, according to the medieval *Lanercost Chronicle*, his body was flayed and sections of his skin kept as souvenirs: Wallace himself took a broad strip "from the head to the heel" to use as a shoulder belt for his sword. For the English, it was a devastating defeat.

Wallace and Moray became the guardians of the kingdom of Scotland on behalf of the incarcerated John Balliol, but Moray soon succumbed to wounds he had suffered in the battle, leaving Wallace as the figurehead of the resistance. He was knighted for his efforts and continued to harry the English, even leading raids into northern England.

## FAILURE AT FALKIRK

With the future of Scotland now at stake, Edward I marched on the kingdom in 1298. Wallace continued to prove himself a master tactician and refused to engage the superior force in full-on battle. He drew Edward farther

and farther into Scotland, laying waste to the countryside so that the English could not restock their provisions. However, in July 1298 informants had told Edward of the exact position of Wallace's army near Falkirk, and he launched a surprise, full-scale attack on July 22. Again outnumbered, with only 6,000 men to Edward's 15,000, Wallace could not hold out this time, especially under the onslaught of the English archers.

After the defeat Wallace resigned the guardianship in favor of Robert Bruce and John Comyn, and the mysterious warrior again disappeared from view. It seems likely that he went abroad to seek support in Europe and did not return until 1303–4. Bruce and Comyn brokered a temporary peace with Edward, but the king still wanted revenge on Wallace for the humiliation at Stirling Bridge.

## HANGED, DRAWN, AND QUARTERED

IN 1351, execution by being hanged, drawn, and quartered became the statutory penalty for high treason in England, but it was already in use by the thirteenth century. Accused who were found guilty of plotting against the monarch endured a public death specifically designed to be both painful and humiliating. The victim would be hanged but taken down while alive so they could witness their own debasement: their genitals would be cut off and they would be "drawn" (disemboweled), beheaded, and "quartered" (chopped into four sections). The pieces would be displayed in public. The practice was abolished only in 1870. Women were spared the ordeal and burned at the stake instead.

## HERO DESPITE HUMILIATION

With a large reward on his head, William Wallace was captured near Glasgow on August 5, 1305. He was charged with treason, which he denied, saying, "I could not be a traitor to Edward, for I was never his subject." Nonetheless, he was sentenced and the horrors of his execution began.

Edward may have thought the rebellion was over, but Bruce would emerge as another champion of independence, defeating the English at Bannockburn in 1314, and the English were forced to acknowledge Scottish independence fifteen years later. Wallace and Bruce remain the two greatest heroes of Scottish history, well after the countries were constitutionally united in 1707. ✿

**Above and opposite:** After being found guilty of treachery by the English court, William Wallace was dragged to Smithfield to be hanged, drawn, and quartered.

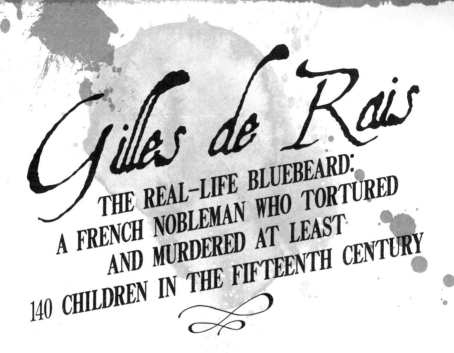

# Gilles de Rais

## THE REAL-LIFE BLUEBEARD: A FRENCH NOBLEMAN WHO TORTURED AND MURDERED AT LEAST 140 CHILDREN IN THE FIFTEENTH CENTURY

Gilles de Rais absorbed the words of Jean de Malestroit, the bishop of Nantes, and trembled with fear. "Milord Gilles de Rais, knight, lord, and baron, our subject and under our jurisdiction, with certain accomplices, did cut the throats of, kill, and heinously massacre many young and innocent boys, that he did practice with these children unnatural lust and the vice of sodomy, often calls up or causes others to practice the dreadful invocation of demons, did sacrifice to and make pacts with the latter, and did perpetrate other enormous crimes." The brave knight and religious scion, who had ridden into battle with Joan of Arc to save Orléans just eleven years earlier, had

finally been exposed. The legend of a real-life monster, one of the worst child killers in history, was born.

Gilles de Rais could not have been born into more advantageous circumstances. In fact, the nobleman claimed that this was the very thing that had uncoupled his reason: at his execution, as he faced the noose, he gave a sermon on the evils of an overly privileged, ill-disciplined upbringing. Gilles's ability to fulfill with ease even the wildest dreams of the common man had pushed him beyond the borders of sanity and into a realm of extraordinary depravity.

He was born Gilles de Montmorency-Laval at the family estate of Champtocé-sur-Loire, France, around September 1405, taking the title Baron Gilles de Rais (or de Retz) after the early death of his wealthy father. He married young, at the age of 15, to the heiress Catherine de Thouars of Brittany,

## ❧ FACT FILE ❧

**Born:** c. September 1405, Champtocé-sur-Loire.

**Died:** October 25, 1440, Nantes.

**Historic Feat:** Helped to defeat the English in the Hundred Years' War but went on to murder 140 children.

**Circumstances of Death:** Tried by a joint ecclesiastical and secular court and hanged.

**Legacy:** Thought to have inspired the French folktale of Bluebeard, the serial wife-killer.

**Opposite:** A nineteenth-century engraving of the mass murderer Gilles de Rais callously experimenting on one of his young victims.

increasing his fortune still further. However, Gilles was not content to waste away in pampered affluence and chose to fight for king and country.

## NATIONAL HERO

From 1427 to 1435 he was a commander in the royal army of the dauphin Charles in the war with England and Burgundy, and repeatedly distinguished himself with acts of bravery. In 1429, he played a part in the relief of Orléans from an English siege, which paved the way for the dauphin to become Charles VII of France. He was granted the esteemed title of marshal of France for his endeavors. To France he was a hero, and he showed every sign of religious piety too, constructing his own Chapel of the Holy Innocents and supporting a coterie of priests and choristers.

However, after his retirement from martial life in 1435, he would be accused of satanic practices and of the ritual murder of children. Many peasant boys had started to disappear, but in a tale that pre-empts that of Elizabeth Báthory (1560–1614), the serial-killing Blood Countess, no action was taken until a crime was committed against a person of greater standing. Only then were the voices of the peasant children's parents heard.

## POWERFUL ENEMY

Gilles' great mistake occurred on May 15, 1440, when, during a property dispute with the duke of Brittany, he kidnapped the priest of the Church of St. Étienne-de-

**Right:** Gilles de Rais was a companion of Joan of Arc and a French military hero before becoming infamous as one of the most prolific child killers in history.

Mer-Morte, who was the brother of Brittany's treasurer. This led to an investigation by the bishop of Nantes, who then gave credence to ongoing rumors that the baron was responsible for the disappearance of local children and heretical behavior. At first Gilles refused to answer the resultant charges, which included the murder of 140 children and summoning demons, and was excommunicated.

The inquisition allowed evidence to be heard from

Gilles's accomplices as well as the victims' families. The first of many child victims was reported to be Jeudon, a ferrier's boy who had been sent to deliver a message to Gilles's residence at Machecoul. He never returned. Poitou, Gilles's servant and accomplice, revealed that the baron would first of all pamper his young victims, feeding them and dressing them in finery before the games began. He would then hang the children from a hook and masturbate on their bellies before he or one of his accomplices killed them by slitting their throats, beheading them, or breaking their necks, and dismembering them.

Gilles refused to admit to any satanic practices and offered to take an ordeal by fire to prove his innocence. However, facing torture, Gilles confessed to the murders in graphic detail, revealing that he would kiss the dead victims and take great pleasure in looking at their severed limbs and the exposed organs of their eviscerated bodies. Poitou and another servant would then burn the bodies. The last of the victims of one of the worst child killers in history was dispatched in August 1440.

Gilles was sentenced to death by hanging, but he pleaded to be restored to the church. As the baron had not confessed to heresy, the bishop of Nantes agreed, thereby allowing Gilles to be buried on hallowed ground. On October 25, Gilles was hanged, but his body was spared incineration by a fire.

Doubts persist over Gilles's guilt, as the duke of Brittany, who allowed the prosecution, stood to gain Gilles's lands after his conviction, while Gilles himself may have confessed purely to avoid both torture and excommunication. The French folktale of Bluebeard, in which a violent nobleman kills his wives, is said to derive from the story of the mass-murdering Gilles de Rais, not least because he supposedly had a blue-black beard. ⚙

## ORDEAL BY FIRE

GILLES de Rais wished to prove his innocence of summoning demons by undergoing ordeal by fire, even though it could have killed him. In the Middle Ages, the ordeal could involve walking on heated plow shares, holding a hot iron poker, or removing a stone from boiling oil, lead, or water. Innocence would be proved by remaining unharmed. The excommunicated Dominican friar Girolamo Savonarola tried to prove the sanctity of his religious mission by promising to walk through fire in 1498. A torrential downpour extinguished the flames, which confirmed to onlookers that the priest was a heretic. Consequently he was tortured, hanged, and torched.

# Vlad the Impaler

## THE FIFTEENTH-CENTURY EAST EUROPEAN RULER WHO ENJOYED TORTURING AND IMPALING HIS VICTIMS

"He roasted children, whom he fed to their mothers. And cut off the breasts of women, and forced their husbands to eat them. After that, he had them all impaled." So claimed a sixteenth-century German pamphlet, doubtless in a fit of exaggeration, about the infamous Vlad the Impaler. Nonetheless, Vlad was a mass murderer responsible for repulsive scenes of carnage, including that of a forest of stakes, each one impaling a different human victim, with some no doubt still twitching and moaning.

Vlad the Impaler's proper title was Vlad III of Wallachia but he was rechristened by chroniclers in response to his preferred method of killing his enemies: pinning the living victim to a stake. The other name by which he was known would also cause panic and fear for centuries to come: Dracula.

**Opposite:** A sixteenth-century portrait of Vlad the Impaler, otherwise known as Dracula, who inspired Bram Stoker's tale of a vampiric killer.

## FACT FILE

**Born:** c. November 1431, Sighișoara.

**Died:** c. December 1476, Wallachia.

**Historic Feat:** Defeated the Ottomans; responsible for at least 80,000 impalements.

**Circumstances of Death:** Killed in battle by the Ottomans.

**Legacy:** The inspiration for Count Dracula, also remembered as the merciless Vlad the Impaler.

## "SON OF THE DRAGON"

Vlad was born into a royal family in Transylvania (in modern-day Romania) in 1431. His father, Vlad II, ruled the neighboring territory of Wallachia and was known as Vlad Dracul—which means "Vlad the Dragon"—after he was inducted into the Order of the Dragon.

The word "Dracul" had far from satanic connotations: the order was a chivalric body of Christian knights who were committed to defending the faith, and their territories, from the onslaught from the Muslim Ottoman Turks who had spread their empire westward into Europe from modern-day Turkey. Vlad Dracula simply meant Vlad "son of the Dragon," and he would take up his father's cause, join the same order, and attempt to repel the Ottomans.

As Vlad would become known for his mercilessness and sadism, the name Dracula became associated

with evil and was used as a suggestive moniker for the vampire of Irish author Bram Stoker's popular novel, published in 1897. The real and fictional Draculas, however, were worlds apart: Stoker's vampire bit the necks of a few comely maidens; the Impaler murdered at least 80,000 people and was responsible for the demise of many more through the razing of villages and crops.

The Impaler's father, Vlad II, who was at war with the local nobility, the boyars, relied on Ottoman support to keep the throne of Wallachia. In return he had to pay tribute to the Muslim sultan and allow two of his younger sons, Vlad and Radu, to become hostages of the Ottoman court in Edirne. Vlad was well educated during his three years at court, but was frequently beaten and whipped for his arrogance and defiance. His younger brother Radu, meanwhile, proved to be a court favorite: he later converted to Islam and entered Ottoman service.

Vlad II was killed in 1447 by a combination of John Hunyadi, the ruler of Hungary, and the boyars, who also blinded Vlad's elder brother and buried him alive. The Ottomans responded by invading Wallachia and putting the new heir, Vlad III, on the throne. He was just 16 and was soon ousted by John Hunyadi, who made his own ally, Vladislav II, the ruler of the principality of Wallachia.

After first fleeing to Moldavia, Vlad ended up under the protection of John's own court in Hungary, but in 1456, while John attacked the Ottomans in Serbia and ultimately died, Vlad gathered a force to retake the throne of Wallachia. He killed Vladislav himself in close combat.

Vlad, despite his wider reputation for malevolence, remains a folk hero among Romanians for his reparation of Wallachia and his wars against the Ottomans. The region was in a crippled state after decades of conflict when Vlad returned, but his administrative skills combined with utter ruthlessness rebuilt the territory. He decreed severe

punishments to restore law and order, and killed dozens of boyars, whom he held responsible for much of the turmoil. His personal army, made up of menacing mercenaries, raided Transylvania and wiped out Saxon settlers. Vlad's innovative execution technique of impaling victims on a forest of stakes became a favored tool.

**Above and opposite:** Soon after Vlad's death, his gory mass murders were depicted in German woodcuts, including one of him dining amongst a forest of impaled victims while other bodies are dismembered.

## DEFYING THE OTTOMANS

With local enemies quelled, Vlad Dracula turned his attention to the Ottoman Empire. Vlad refused to pay Sultan Mehmet II's tribute in 1459, and nailed the turbans of his Ottoman envoys to their heads. Mehmet's

**Above:** Even during his own lifetime, Vlad was so reviled that his features were used in depictions of Christ's enemies, such as Pontius Pilate.
**Opposite:** Bran Castle, also known as Dracula's Castle, in modern-day Romania on the former border of Wallachia and Transylvania.

response was to send a huge army to defeat him, but the Wallachians surrounded the Ottoman cavalry of 10,000 as they rode through a narrow pass and captured almost the entire force. The prisoners were all impaled on stakes and left to die.

Three years later, Vlad took his army across the river Danube to lay waste to Ottoman-held land. He was proud of the slaughter, writing to the king of Hungary, Matthias Corvinus, that he had "killed peasants, men and women, young and old … We killed 23,884 Turks without counting those we burned in homes or those whose heads were cut off by our soldiers." It is a disturbingly precise figure, revealing Vlad's personal attention to the details of the bloodbath.

In spring 1462 Mehmet duly sent a force of 90,000 men to obliterate Vlad's army. Yet this army was defeated by a force half its size. As had become usual, ritual evisceration and mass murder followed. It is said that the sultan fled to Constantinople in recoil after witnessing the sight of 20,000 Turks impaled on an apparently endless field of stakes.

It was left to Radu, Vlad's younger brother, to defeat Dracula later in 1462. Vlad's resources were weakened following the Ottoman battles earlier that year, while Radu had a fresh supply of the famed Ottoman Janissary troops and the remaining rebellious local boyars at his disposal. After defeating Vlad at his stronghold of Poenari Castle, Radu was made the *bey* or district governor of Wallachia under the authority of the sultan.

Vlad fled to Hungary to seek financial and military assistance from Matthias Corvinus, who had been given papal funds to arrest the disturbing westward creep of the Muslim empire. However, the wary Hungarian imprisoned Vlad III in Buda for ten years. When Radu suddenly died in 1475, Vlad attempted to return to the throne of Wallachia once more but he was killed in battle by Ottoman forces, probably toward the end of 1476, although the exact date and location remain unknown. His head was carried back to Constantinople in triumph.

## LEGEND OF DRACULA

Woodcuts, pamphlets, and poems about the exploits of the mad Dracula started to appear in Germany even before his death, helping to establish the legend of Vlad the Impaler. Meanwhile, Matthias Corvinus sought to discredit Vlad in order to explain his reluctance to aid the Wallachians in the war against the Ottomans in 1462. In time, Vlad became known more for his use of mass torture and as the inspiration for Bram Stoker's *Dracula* than as the attempted savior of Wallachia and scourge of the Ottomans.

Wallachia remained part of the Ottoman Empire until the nineteenth century and is now a region of Romania. ⚙

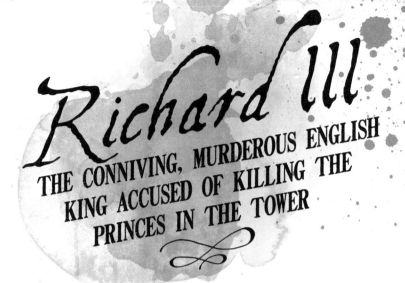

# Richard III
## THE CONNIVING, MURDEROUS ENGLISH KING ACCUSED OF KILLING THE PRINCES IN THE TOWER

At the pivotal moment of the battle, the king of England led a mounted charge straight at Henry Tudor, his rival for the crown. It was a foolhardy maneuver because Henry was surrounded by his best knights and soldiers, but the situation was desperate and Richard III was nothing if not brave. The battle-hardened warrior-king slew Henry's standard-bearer and knocked Sir John Cheyne, an acclaimed jouster, from his horse. Richard was almost within striking distance of Henry himself when his horse became mired in the boggy battlefield and Henry Tudor's men closed in on him.

It was not a noble execution: Richard suffered ten wounds, eight

**Opposite:** A late sixteenth-century portrait of Richard III, the infamous monarch who became the final king of England to die in battle.

### ⤲ FACT FILE ⤲

**Born:** October 2, 1452, Northamptonshire.

**Died:** August 22, 1485, Bosworth Field.

**Historic Feat:** Plotted and murdered his way to becoming king of England.

**Circumstances of Death:** Slain at the Battle of Bosworth Field against Henry VII.

**Legacy:** Made significant judicial reforms but caricatured as a power-hungry, murderous hunchback.

of them to his head. The lacerations were inflicted by arrow, sword, and dagger, but the death blow came from a halberd, a sharp, curved ax blade mounted on a long pole. It was struck with such violence that a section of the king's skull was sheared from the back of his head and his brain was exposed to the air.

Any idea that Richard was a good king seeped away into the mud of the battlefield. Over the course of the ensuing centuries, he would be portrayed as one of the vilest kings in history, a twisted, treacherous, power-crazed hunchback who would stop at nothing, including the infanticide of his own relatives, to seize power. Richard *did* suffer from a minor curvature to his spine—the unearthing of his remains in 2012 proved as much—but history has contorted the image of the man more than Nature ever did.

He was a ruthless killer, but he was

**Above:** The Yorkist victory at the Battle of Barnet in 1471.

**Opposite:** A Victorian depiction of the murder of the Princes in the Tower in 1483; Princes Edward and Richard mysteriously disappeared and are believed to have been murdered on the orders of their own uncle, the power-hungry Richard III.

born in a time of killing. Richard was born at Fotheringay Castle in England on October 2, 1452, on the cusp of one of the most tempestuous eras in British history: the Wars of the Roses between the Yorkists and the Lancastrians. By the time he was eight, both his father, Richard Plantagenet, a Yorkist claimant to the throne, and one of his brothers had been killed in battle. His own safety only became more assured after the Lancastrian king, Henry VI, had been defeated in 1461 and Richard's eldest brother became Edward IV, the first Yorkist monarch.

## RISE TO POWER

Still a child, Richard was made duke of Gloucester and began his intensive training to become a warrior-knight. A clever, brave, and capable boy, Richard was commanding his own force by the time he was 17, but in 1470 he and King Edward IV were forced to flee abroad owing to the treachery of their brother, the duke of Clarence, and their previous ally, the earl of Warwick. Henry VI, now an old man suffering from bouts of insanity, was returned to the throne, but Warwick was king in all but name.

Edward and Richard had no intention of accepting their fate and Clarence, meanwhile, had realized the folly of his allegiance with Warwick and switched sides again. Luck was on the brothers' side when they returned to England in 1470 and engaged Warwick's forces at the Battle of Barnet in April 1471. In dense fog and the chaos of battle, a section of the Lancastrian army was slaughtered by their own forces and the Yorkists seized the initiative. Warwick attempted to flee the battlefield, but he was unhorsed and slain.

Henry VI was imprisoned in the Tower of London and his son, Edward, the Prince of Wales, was defeated at the Battle of Tewkesbury in May 1471. The prince and many more Lancastrian supporters were killed in battle or dragged from their homes and slaughtered in the aftermath, and Richard would have played his part.

## DARK DEEDS IN THE TOWER

A fortnight later, Henry VI mysteriously died in the Tower of London. The author of the *Historie of the Arivall of Edward IV* claimed that cause of death was "displeasure and melancholy." The future chancellor of Henry VIII,

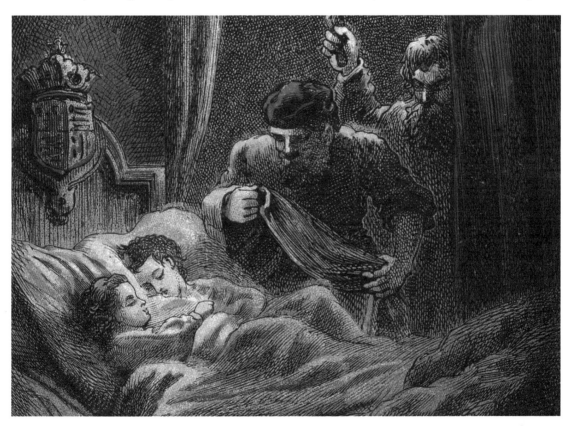

## MURDER IN THE TOWER

THE Tower of London may be more famous as a prison and the scene of executions, but it was first built by William the Conqueror in the 1090s as a fortress and royal residence. When its most famous residents, the young King Edward V and his brother Richard—"the princes in the Tower"—were incarcerated there in 1483, they would have lived in luxury, not in a dungeon. The Tudors used the Tower more frequently as a prison, especially Elizabeth I, who sent numerous enemies there for torture and execution. Tools of torture used at the Tower included the rack and the scavenger's daughter, a torture machine whose name is a corrupted form of its inventor Sir William Skeffington.

Thomas More, preferred to blame Richard—who was still only 18—claiming in his *History of King Richard III* that Richard killed him with his own hand. English playwright William Shakespeare saw dramatic potential in regicide and murder, and in his work the deaths of Prince Edward and, later, Clarence, were added to the litany of Richard's villainous acts—all without a shred of evidence.

Whatever the truth, the Lancastrians were no more. Edward IV should have been able to rule in peace, with Richard and Clarence at his side. Richard even married Warwick's daughter, Ann, but this did not help smooth the path to a sustained peace. The bloodshed was far from over. Clarence, perhaps the single most untrustworthy man in an era of untrustworthy men, was soon flexing his muscles again and was beheaded in 1478 for treason.

Richard, acting in the king's interests, proved himself to be an able administrator in the north and a keen advocate of the rights of the common man before the law. However, with the death of Edward IV in 1483, he felt he had served his apprenticeship and began a series of Machiavellian maneuvers that would fuel his later detractors. He was appointed Lord Protector on behalf of Edward's son, the 12-year-old Edward V, and with the help of the duke of Buckingham began to remove—by means of arrest, imprisonment, and execution—all threats to his power. These included his nephews—the young Edward and his brother Richard—who were taken to reside in the Tower of London "for their own protection." Richard then contrived to have them declared illegitimate and was crowned king himself.

**Opposite:** Richard III riding toward certain death at the Battle of Bosworth Field, 1485.

The princes in the Tower mysteriously disappeared—presumed killed at Richard's behest. Buckingham turned on the new king and led an unsuccessful rebellion to put Henry Tudor on the throne. Tudor's tenuous claim to the throne was through an illegitimate female line, but there was sufficient groundswell of support to mount another serious challenge in 1485. Richard had been on the throne for just two years when he faced Tudor at Bosworth Field. He initially had the larger force, but some of his allies switched sides, leading Richard to shout "Treason!" before he hurled himself straight into the ranks of the enemy in order to kill Henry himself. He was the last king of England to die in battle.

As the cliché goes, history is written by the victors. Henry VII's dubious claim to the throne made it particularly important for the Tudor dynasty to defame the man from whom they had torn the crown. Contemporary chronicler John Rous, who had called Richard a good lord who defended the common people, now claimed that Richard was a freakish, deformed monster kept in the womb for two years before birth. Thomas More joined the smear campaign, and in c. 1592 in *The Tragedy of King Richard III* Shakespeare conjured a portrait of a tyrannical villain, having Richard describe himself as "Cheated of feature by dissembling nature,/Deform'd, unfinish'd, sent before my time/Into this breathing world, scarce half made up."

Richard is indubitably the victim of an historical conceit, but he was far from saintly and the ghosts of his two young nephews will always hamper any fulsome restoration of his reputation. ⚙

# Guy Fawkes

## THE ROMAN CATHOLIC WHO TRIED TO SET FIRE TO THE ENGLISH PARLIAMENT IN 1605 AND WAS TORTURED ON THE RACK

On November 5, 1605, Guy Fawkes stood in the candlelight of the underground cellar, checking for a final time that the barrels of gunpowder were carefully hidden by the piles of wood and coal. He felt the rough hemp of the fuse between his fingers. It was past midnight and later that day, immediately above the cellar, King James I would be adjusting his robes and taking his place on the throne for the opening of Parliament. Guy Fawkes, meanwhile, would be standing in the cellar once more, holding the same fuse, but this time he would be lighting it, and the king and all the Protestant nobles would be blasted to damnation.

As he left the cellar, the quiet underground vaults were suddenly filled with the sound of boots stomping on stone and men shouting with urgency. Fawkes turned quickly, thinking that he could still light the fuse and raze the Houses of Parliament to the ground, but the guards were already upon him, pulling him away. As they dragged him out of the building, he knew that his own death was now certain. The most

**Right:** The Gunpowder Plot conspirators, based on a contemporary engraving: Robert Catesby and Guy Fawkes are second and third from the right.

### ⌘ FACT FILE ⌘

**Born:** April 15, 1570, York.
**Died:** January 31, 1606, London.
**Historic Feat:** Attempted to bring Roman Catholicism back to England by trying to blow up Parliament and kill the king.
**Circumstances of Death:** Arrested, tried for high treason, and hanged.
**Legacy:** The plot failed and the Protestant Church of England remains the official religion.

daring assassination attempt in the history of England had just been foiled.

Guy Fawkes was not born a Roman Catholic but he would spend his life fighting and killing on behalf of the faith. Born on April 15, 1570, in York in northern England, he took up the religion after his father died and his mother married a devout Catholic. England had been in religious turmoil since 1534. King Henry VIII, who was a follower of Protestant theology and at odds with the Roman Catholic Church due to his wish to divorce his wife, had decreed that England was to be a Protestant country: religious tolerance was abandoned and Catholics were forced to attend Protestant Church of England services by law. Roman Catholics had been persecuted ever since, with the brief exception of the reign of Mary I (1553–58), a Catholic who meted out revenge with such alacrity that she became known as "Bloody Mary." Ever since her death, fervent Catholics had been plotting to restore a Catholic to the throne, but the Gunpowder Plot was the most ambitious conspiracy of them all.

In 1591, at the age of 21, Fawkes left for the European mainland to fight on behalf of Roman Catholic Spain against the Protestant Dutch Republic, despite the fact that Spain was an enduring enemy of England. Many of Fawkes's devout Catholic acquaintances in England had been thrown into prison, so he felt no loyalty to his country. He spent most of the next twelve years fighting for Spain and even managed to gain access to the Spanish court, where he failed to convince King Philip III to support a Catholic rebellion in England. By this time James I, a Protestant Scot, was on the throne of England and continuing to support anti-Catholic laws.

## CATESBY CONSPIRACY

By 1604, Fawkes was back in England and had joined a group of rebellious conspirators led by a nobleman named Robert

Catesby. Together they hatched a plan to assassinate James I and exterminate the Protestant aristocracy. Simultaneously, they would kidnap King James's daughter, the 9-year-old Princess Elizabeth, and place her on the throne as a Catholic monarch. The conspirators rented a house near Parliament and started to dig a tunnel beneath the House of Lords so that they could lay explosives under the building. They abandoned this plan when, by chance, they learned that they could hire a recently vacated undercroft directly underneath Parliament.

In summer 1605 the plotters secretly amassed about three dozen barrels of gunpowder in the cellar, which they would ignite on November 5, the first day of the new session of Parliament. However, the plotters did not wish to kill any devout Roman Catholics in the explosion, so they sent anonymous letters to a few chosen noblemen, warning them to stay away from the opening of Parliament.

Guy Fawkes was put in charge of the gunpowder and the conspirators chose him to ignite the huge explosion. He had been checking the hoard for a final time when the king's men searched the cellars, arrested him, and found the gunpowder. Robert Cecil, the king's spymaster, had been tipped off about the plot by William Parker, 4th Baron Montague, who was one of the Catholic noblemen who had received a warning letter from the conspirators. Cecil was already aware of Fawkes's anti-Protestant activities through his network of spies in Europe.

## TORTURE AND SENTENCING

Fawkes said his name was John Johnson and confessed that he had intended to blow up the Houses of Parliament, but claimed that he was working alone. He needed to protect Catesby and his fellow conspirators who were simultaneously attempting to raise a rebellion in the Midlands, which would have been triggered by the death of the king. King James

himself decided that torture would loosen Fawkes's tongue. He was taken to the Tower of London and tied to the rack. During the course of several days of excruciating pain, his resolve was broken: he told the interrogators his real name and those of his conspirators. Catesby and the Midlands contingent were hunted down and killed, and Catesby's decapitated head was placed on the side of the Parliament building in London.

Fawkes and the remaining conspirators were found guilty of high treason and sentenced to be hanged, drawn, and quartered on January 31, 1606. After the hanging, they would still be alive when they were disemboweled. Fawkes,

**Opposite:** The arrest of Guy Fawkes and discovery of the cache of gunpowder under the Houses of Parliament.
**Above:** The anti-Catholic King James I with his consort, Anne of Denmark.

the last to be hanged, was still weak and stumbling from the effects of torture, but, with the noose around his throat, he managed to throw himself from the gallows so that his neck broke, killing him immediately.

An Act of Parliament soon decreed that November 5 should be celebrated every year as "the joyful day of deliverance." A tradition of lighting bonfires immediately began, which became augmented by the burning of an effigy of the pope and lighting fireworks as the seventeenth century

**Below:** The execution of Guy Fawkes and his fellow conspirators in 1606, depicted at the time by Claes Jansz Visscher.

**Opposite:** Guy Fawkes's letter of confession, extracted after he was tortured on the rack.

progressed. "Guy Fawkes' Night" is still celebrated annually and today the effigy is usually of Guy Fawkes himself.

The Gunpowder Plot achieved nothing for the fortunes of Roman Catholicism in England and merely increased the distrust with which Catholics were treated. After James II, who became king of England in 1685, revealed that he was a Catholic and tried to put in place measures of religious tolerance, he was unceremoniously deposed. William of Orange, who had a lesser claim on the throne, was invited to invade England solely because he was a fervent anti-Catholic. There has not been another Roman Catholic ruler of England ever since and the Act of Settlement, passed in 1701, still prevents any Catholic or even anyone married to a Catholic from acceding to the throne. ☼

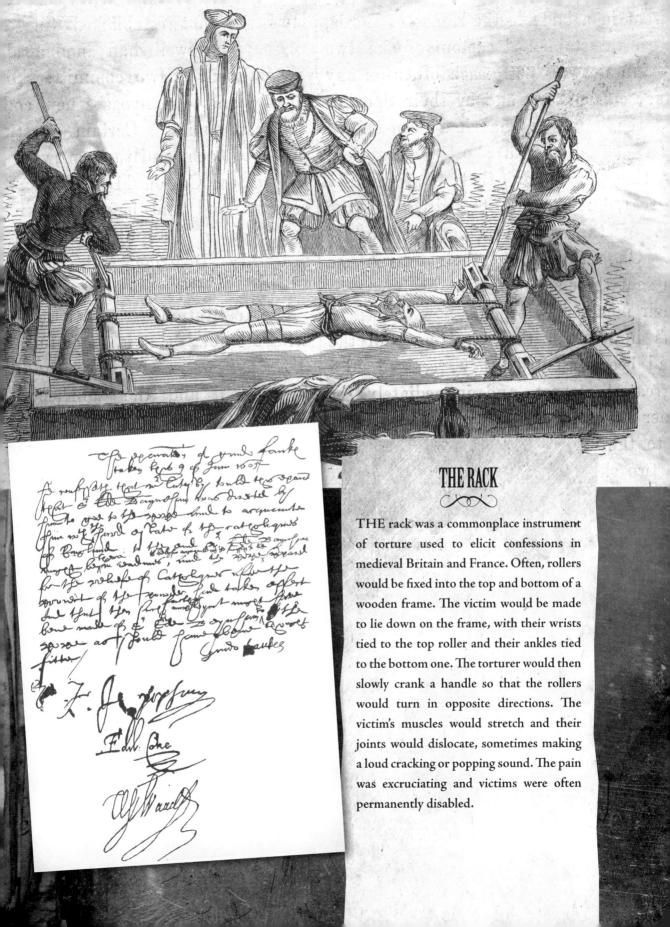

## THE RACK

THE rack was a commonplace instrument of torture used to elicit confessions in medieval Britain and France. Often, rollers would be fixed into the top and bottom of a wooden frame. The victim would be made to lie down on the frame, with their wrists tied to the top roller and their ankles tied to the bottom one. The torturer would then slowly crank a handle so that the rollers would turn in opposite directions. The victim's muscles would stretch and their joints would dislocate, sometimes making a loud cracking or popping sound. The pain was excruciating and victims were often permanently disabled.

# Benedict Arnold

## THE TRAITOROUS AMERICAN WHO ATTEMPTED TO HELP THE BRITISH IN THE AMERICAN WAR OF INDEPENDENCE

He had been humiliated and his pride was scorched. Time and again, he had been slighted—even though he had given everything for the cause of his embryonic country. He had put his life on the line and even sacrificed his leg. Now, he was a cripple who doubted he would have any future chance of riches or real power. If he stayed true to the cause. He picked up the pen and wrote swiftly, angrily, spurred on by the memory of each blow from his so-called allies who had demeaned him or held him back, and later thrust the documents into the hands of his accomplice, John André. Benedict Arnold, American patriot, had just sold his soul to the enemy by formulating a plot to surrender the fort at West Point at a crucial time in the American War of Independence. He would be known as one of the worst traitors in American history.

Arnold was an unlikely villain. He was born in Norwich, Connecticut, in 1741, a descendant of John Lothropp, a clergyman whose more loyal descendants would include six U.S. presidents, notably Franklin D. Roosevelt. While he was a child, his family moved in esteemed social circles, but his father's alcoholism and increasing penury curtailed Arnold's private education. Arnold made his own fortune as an owner of merchant ships, but he suffered at the hands of punishing British taxation of the American colonies and had trouble with creditors.

He gave sure signs of being a future patriot, joining the secret Sons of Liberty organization to defy British rule. After the Boston Massacre of 1770, when British soldiers killed five civilians, Benedict

**Opposite:** After his treachery was discovered, Benedict Arnold escaped from West Point and joined the British forces.

## ⬥ FACT FILE ⬥

**Born:** January 14, 1741, Norwich, Connecticut.
**Died:** June 14, 1801, London.
**Historic Feat:** Betrayed America to the British in the War of Independence.
**Circumstances of Death:** Died of illness having moved to London.
**Legacy:** One of the most infamous traitors in American history.

wrote, "are the Americans all asleep and tamely giving up their liberties, or are they all turned philosophers, that they don't take immediate vengeance on such miscreants?"

## MILITARY PROWESS

When the War of Independence broke out in 1775, he was a captain in the Connecticut militia. He helped lead Ethan Hale's Green Mountain Boys in the successful capture of Fort Ticonderoga, New York, in May of that year, and showed tactical sensibility even in the defeat at Valcour Island in 1776. Further personal successes followed with his campaign to harass British forces at Ridgeway in 1777. Later that year, on September 19, he served with distinction at the first Battle of Saratoga,

where he pre-empted an enemy flanking maneuver, allowing enough time for American forces to regroup with the aid of reinforcements. Despite his heroism, his commander General Horatio Gates refused to alert the Continental Congress about his role in the battle and then took away his command for insubordination.

This was not the first slight Arnold had suffered in his military career. The Green Mountain Boys had apparently jeered at him despite the victory at Ticonderoga, and he had needed to turn to Congress after the authorities refused to meet his campaign expenses. Then he was arrested, and released, in 1776 during a court case relating to the plundering of Montreal following Arnold's successful evacuation of

the city. Other officers made further charges against him and he was overlooked for high promotion by Congress, despite George Washington's support. After he was finally promoted to major general, he was stripped of his seniority, which angered Arnold greatly.

Despite being demoted by Gates, Arnold took it upon himself to ride straight between the British and American lines at the second Battle of Saratoga, which had reached stalemate, on October 7, 1777. He then led a charge that changed the course of the battle—and the war—allowing the Americans to capture the British position. In the final throes of battle, Arnold was shot in the leg and then broke it when his horse fell on him, and he was bedridden for the next six months. His seniority was restored, but it was Gates who received the accolades for Arnold's actions, which led to British surrender, and he was given the command of the army in the south.

Arnold was crippled and broiling with discontent, but he signed the Oath of Allegiance to his country on May 30, 1778, and Washington made him the commandant of Philadelphia. Having lost his first wife in 1775, Arnold married the young socialite Peggy Shippen but the couple lived beyond their means. Arnold was soon in trouble again, and was successfully court-martialed for using government equipment and passes for his own gain, with Washington publicly rebuking him. By now Arnold was increasingly embittered and turning against his countrymen, having disagreed with the American alliance with France.

**Above and opposite:** The traitor Benedict Arnold was once an American hero who performed valiantly at the Battles of Saratoga in 1777 during the American Revolutionary War.

## INFORMATION FOR SALE

By 1779, Arnold was ready to sell his services to the British in return for huge wealth. He sent a series of coded letters to John André, the chief intelligence officer of the British commander, Sir Henry Clinton. André was an acquaintance of Arnold's wife, and Arnold's letters revealing patriot maneuvers and defenses were passed to the British through Peggy's social circle. In August 1880, Arnold was appointed to a position from which he could greatly influence the outcome of the war in Britain's favor: commander of the fort at West Point. Arnold was offered £20,000 to surrender West Point, which would allow the British to control the all-important Hudson River.

### SPIES OF THE REVOLUTION

JOHN André was one of many spies used by the British in the War of Independence, but the American patriots had their own sophisticated network of agents. As well as Nathan Hale, the national hero executed by the British, and his former classmate, the spymaster Benjamin Tallmadge, the Americans had a ring of spies called the Mechanics, which grew out of the Sons of Liberty organization that once counted the traitor Benedict Arnold amongst its members. The Boston-based Mechanics informed on British maneuvers and stole military equipment. Paul Revere, one of the Mechanics, famously rode through the night, crossing enemy lines, to alert American forces prior to the battles of Lexington and Concord in 1775.

Arnold would be free of the carping, demotions, court cases, and financial problems that had plagued his career. All he had to do was betray the country for which he had fought so valiantly.

In September 1780, Arnold sat down and wrote detailed instructions for the capture of the fort and drew careful plans. He sent André away with the documents along with a pass to ensure the spy's safe passage back to Clinton. André never made it. He was stopped by American soldiers, who found the revealing documents hidden in a stocking. On learning of André's arrest, Arnold suddenly disappeared from West Point and defected to the British.

In return for his duplicity, the British gave him £6,000, land in Canada, and a commission as a brigadier-general in the British army. He led British forces in battle against his fellow Americans, although he could not prevent the enemy's slide to defeat, which eventually came in 1783. By then, Arnold had left America and moved to London, but he was not given a military command. The British never really trusted their turncoat. Consequently he went to Canada and assumed his old trade of merchant shipping, but he was not welcomed with open arms there, either—throughout both his civilian and military careers, Arnold ignited feelings of dislike and distrust amongst his peers. He returned to London in 1791 and again sought military command, but none was forthcoming.

Arnold died in 1801, by then a somewhat obscure figure in his adopted country, but he would remain known for centuries to come as the traitor who had attempted to turn the war in favor of America's great enemy and prevent independence. ✿

**Opposite:** Major John André, Arnold's British accomplice, was caught with Arnold's incriminating papers in his stocking and was hanged as a spy.

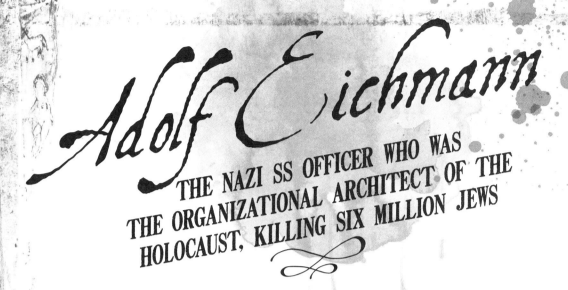

# Adolf Eichmann

## THE NAZI SS OFFICER WHO WAS THE ORGANIZATIONAL ARCHITECT OF THE HOLOCAUST, KILLING SIX MILLION JEWS

Otto Adolf Eichmann—known as Adolf and proud to share his Christian name with the Nazi führer ("leader") Adolf Hitler—called his hand-picked staff into his office in Berlin and said, "I will leap into my grave laughing because the feeling that I have five million human beings on my conscience is for me a source of extraordinary satisfaction." Eichmann had been appointed as the operational mastermind to oversee the wholesale destruction of the Jews in Germany and German-occupied lands. It was a huge task, which he undertook with both diligence and relish, making him responsible for the greatest mass murder in history. Although he never killed a Jew with his own hands, he was the cold,

calculating master of a vast death machine.

Born on March 19, 1906, in Solingen in Germany before his family moved to Austria, Adolf Eichmann was an unremarkable boy who did not excel at school. He worked for his father's mining company before becoming a sales clerk and then a traveling salesman for an oil company. His life would probably have passed without causing a blip in the consciousness of the world had it not been for the rise of Adolf Hitler.

Eichmann had gone to the same Austrian school that Hitler had attended almost two decades earlier and he kept a keen eye on the rapid rise of the extreme national socialist. Hitler's policies chimed with his own desire for a racially pure Greater Germany and the suppression of the Jews. Eichmann became a member of the Nazi Party and joined its feared SS paramilitary (*Schutzstaffel* or "Protection Squad") in 1932. The following year, following the

### ⌘ FACT FILE ⌘

**Born:** March 19, 1906, Solingen.
**Died:** May 31, 1962, Ramia.
**Historic Feat:**
Organized the mass deportation of Jews to Nazi extermination camps in the Second World War.
**Circumstances of Death:**
Hanged in Israel after being found guilty of crimes against humanity.
**Legacy:** The organizational architect of the Holocaust.

**Opposite:** Adolf Eichmann paces his prison yard prior to his trial in Israel, 1961.

Nazi seizure of power in Germany, he lost his job as an oil salesman and returned to his home country. The Nazis recognized his administrative skills and in 1934 he joined the Jewish department, entrusted with helping to ensure that Jews left Germany as a result of economic repression and violent intimidation. At the age of 28, he had found his true—and appalling—vocation. The policies were effective, with 350,000 Jewish people emigrating from Germany and Austria before the outbreak of the Second World War in 1939.

After the German invasion of Poland, Nazi anti-Semitism reached a new phase: rather than waiting for Jews to feel so beleaguered by racial bullying that they would emigrate, they would now be forcibly deported from the land of the Third Reich. By now, Eichmann was

the head of the Central Office for Jewish Emigration, under the supervision of the head of the Gestapo (*Geheime Staatspolizei* or "Secret State Police"). Jews were herded into ghettos and Eichmann created plans for Jewish reservation camps in Poland and even Madagascar to house the deportees as they were forced out of German territories.

## THE FINAL SOLUTION

The plans were never enacted as Nazi policy shifted again to reach the final phase of its evolution in 1941. Deportation was no longer enough: extermination was now the remit. Eichmann and his department were responsible for the deportation of Jews to extermination camps where they would be gassed en masse, while some would also have to endure forced labor or scientific experimentation. Hitler's "Final Solution to the Jewish Question," Eichmann was told, was to kill every Jew on German-occupied land.

Deportation to the initial Nazi death camps at Treblinka, Belzec, and Sobibór in Poland began almost immediately. Eichmann, now promoted to the rank of lieutenant colonel in the SS, collated information on the Jewish population in each targeted sector, had properties seized, and organized the requisite number of trains for the arrested Jews to be deported to the concentration camps. At the Auschwitz-Birkenau camp network, also in Poland, tracks were laid to take the victims within a few hundred yards of the gas chambers.

**Left:** The Red Cross identity document used by Adolf Eichmann to enter Argentina under the assumed name of Ricardo Klement in 1950.
**Opposite:** Eichmann was a proud Nazi who facilitated the mass deportation and extermination of millions of Jews.

Eichmann had already run before then, fleeing to Austria after he had burned all the records of his department. He was not willing to pay for his crimes. He was detained under a false name by U.S. forces, but he eventually made it to Argentina, in 1950, having been furnished with false papers by the Nazi-sympathizer Alois Hudal, an Austrian bishop. By then, Eichmann's terrible crimes had been revealed at the Nuremberg trials of prominent Nazis in November 1945–October 1946 and he was exposed as the operational architect of the genocide.

Mossad, the Israeli secret police, tracked Eichmann down to Buenos Aires in 1960 and kidnapped him. He was illegally smuggled out of Argentina and was found guilty of crimes against humanity at a trial in Israel. He was hanged on May 31, 1962. He never expressed remorse.⚙

## INDUSTRIALIZED MURDER

Eichmann's death machine was well oiled and supremely efficient by the time Germany invaded Hungary on March 19, 1944. Eichmann was present on the day of the invasion, ready to oversee the immediate deportation and extermination of Hungarian Jews. Within just four months, 437,000 Hungarian Jews were killed, mostly at the Auschwitz-Birkenau complex. Four trains, carrying a total of 3,000 Jews, were sent from Hungary to Auschwitz every day. Even when Eichmann was ordered to stop the deportations in July 1944, he sent further trainloads to their deaths. More than 5.5 million Jews were exterminated in camps in eastern Europe during the Second World War.

In April 1945, the Allied forces reached Berlin and the führer shot himself rather than face capture by the Soviets.

## AUSCHWITZ-BIRKENAU

FROM January 1942, Auschwitz, which had previously been used by the Nazis for the internment of Polish political prisoners, was extended to become a huge camp network handling the gassing of Jewish deportees. Over the course of three years, 1.1 million prisoners were killed at the Auschwitz-Birkenau network of camps, mostly through the use of Zyklon B pesticide gas. Others died through starvation and their use as forced labor. Over 900,000 of the dead were Jews, and the remainder were mostly non-Jewish Poles, Soviets, and Romanis. More than 4.5 million Jews were killed at other camps in the Holocaust.

# Pierre Laval

## THE HEAD OF GERMAN-OCCUPIED FRANCE IN THE SECOND WORLD WAR SENT THOUSANDS OF JEWISH CHILDREN TO THEIR DEATHS

Pierre Laval took a gamble that Germany would win the Second World War. It seemed that the odds were in his favor as the Germans had swept through Belgium and most of his own country, France, with comparative ease. The British had tried to turn back the tide in the Battle of France, but that had ended in disaster, and it seemed unlikely that they could muster the resources, or willpower, to attempt a land invasion of German-occupied territory. So Pierre Laval agreed to become the head of the Vichy government of occupied France. Of course, if Germany lost the war, some people might regard him as the worst collaborator and traitor in French history, but surely that would never happen …

**Opposite:** Pierre Laval, the head of the pro-Nazi Vichy government that aided the extermination of Jews, vigorously defended himself against the charge of high treason at his trial in 1945.

Laval, who was born in Châteldon in 1883, was a socialist lawyer but over the years he drifted toward the right. He entered politics in 1914 and went on to hold several positions in government in the 1920s before becoming the prime minister for very short terms in 1931 and 1935.

### FACT FILE

**Born:** June 28, 1883, Châteldon.
**Died:** October 15, 1945, Paris.
**Historic Feat:** French leader who collaborated with the Nazis in the Second World War.
**Circumstances of Death:**
Executed by firing squad, having been found guilty of treason.
**Legacy:** France's most notorious traitor, who collaborated in the extermination of Jewish people, including children.

### COLLABORATOR

In July 1940, Germany proved victorious in the Battle of France, and Laval helped to persuade the French government to agree to an armistice with the aggressors. He became the minister of state in Marshal Philippe Pétain's Vichy government, which only maintained sovereignty over southern France while the Germans occupied the north. Meanwhile, a rival government-in exile, the Free French of General Charles de Gaulle, was set up in London. Laval was convinced that Germany could not be beaten so, rather than continuing to resist the

the German war effort. In return for every three laborers received, one French prisoner of war would be returned.

Laval's greatest crime, though, would be to allow the deportation of Jews to the death camps. He compromised with the Germans, preventing most Jewish French nationals from being deported, but he allowed the extermination of non-nationals living within France's borders, and the French authorities themselves conducted the Jewish manhunts in southern France. In total, the Vichy government was responsible for sending 75,000 Jews to be exterminated. Furthermore, Laval went beyond the agreement, which did not include Jews under the age of 16, and sent children to their deaths.

In the end, Laval's gamble to support the Germans did not pay off. In summer 1944, following the D-Day landings, the Allies swept the German forces out of northern France, French citizens turned on the Vichy collaborators and Laval fled first to Germany and then Spain. However, he never felt that he had betrayed his country and dared to return to defend himself in July 1945. The Free French were not intent on giving a Nazi collaborator—who had aided the German war effort, allowed the oppression of his own people, and abetted the extermination of Jews—anything other than the death sentence.

At 8:45 a.m. on October 15, 1945, the procurator general and Laval's legal team went to his cell in the suburbs of Paris to inform him that his execution by firing squad would go ahead at 9:30 a.m. Laval, who was still in bed, merely put his head under his blanket and said nothing. One of the team eventually pulled the blanket down and saw that Laval was losing consciousness. There was a bottle of potassium cyanide in his hand.

Laval had left a letter at his bedside: "I refuse to be killed by French bullets. I will not make French soldiers

occupation, he decreed that it was best to collaborate with the Nazis in order to protect the future of France. He began to negotiate behind the back of his premier, and handed over control of copper mines as well as the Belgian gold reserves. He was consequently dismissed for his treachery in December 1940.

When Laval returned to become the head of the government in 1942, he was little more than Germany's puppet. In a move that appalled his countrymen, he agreed to send hundreds of thousands of French laborers to help

**Above:** A 1943 cartoon depicting Laval as a puppet of the Nazis.
**Opposite:** Vidkun Quisling shakes the hand of Adolf Hitler at a reception in February 1942.

accomplices in a judicial murder. I have chosen my death—the poison of the Romans, which I have carried with me through my long wanderings and which has escaped the searchings of my guards. I wish to be buried with the Tricolor scarf round my neck. I die because I loved my country too much. My last thought is for France."

The traitor had chosen to kill himself rather than face execution, but he did not succeed. The medics rushed to save him and repeatedly pumped his stomach.

All the commotion managed to achieve was a delay of three hours. At 12:32, Laval stood before the firing squad that had arrived from nearby Fort Châtillon. He wore his trademark white tie and had been allowed to wear the Tricolor around his neck. He had refused a blindfold. He addressed his final words to the soldiers: "I pity you for having to execute this crime. Aim at my heart. Long live France!" The firing squad did its duty and the greatest traitor in French history fell to the ground. To this day, France carries the burden of what happened to the Jews under Laval's premiership. ✿

## VIDKUN QUISLING

VIDKUN Quisling (1887–1945), like France's Pierre Laval, collaborated with the Nazis during the Second World War. While Germany invaded Norway in April 1940, Quisling conducted a coup d'état and became the head of the government. To the disgust of most Norwegian citizens, he allowed the deportation of Jews, army officers, and students, and attempted to force children to join a Nazi Youth-style organization. At the end of the war he was tried for murder, embezzlement, and conspiring with Hitler. He was executed by firing squad on October 24, 1945. The word "quisling" has passed into the English language to describe a person who collaborates with an enemy-occupying force.

# Lavrentiy Beria

## JOSEPH STALIN'S BLOODHOUND, RESPONSIBLE FOR THE EXECUTION OF THOUSANDS OF POLITICAL OPPONENTS IN THE SOVIET UNION

Lavrentiy Beria had chosen the wrong side. In the Russian civil war following the revolutions of 1917 he had failed to continue to support the communist Bolsheviks, who set up the Russian government, and instead had become a spy for their opponents in Azerbaijan, the Muslim Democrat Musavat Party. By 1920, at the age of 21, Beria was already a sly, self-serving careerist lacking a moral compass: he was working for the security department of the anti-Bolshevik Mensheviks in Georgia, but may also have been an agent of the British intelligence service. Beria cursed his mistake later that year when the Musavats were defeated by the Bolsheviks and he was arrested.

**Opposite:** Lavrentiy Beria and Joseph Stalin in 1936. Beria enjoyed torturing opponents on behalf of the Soviet leader.

### FACT FILE

**Born:** March 29, 1899, Gulripshi.

**Died:** December 23, 1953, Moscow.

**Historic Feat:** Organized mass exterminations and deportations on behalf of Joseph Stalin.

**Circumstances of Death:** Denounced and shot as a traitor to the Soviet Union.

**Legacy:** Remembered as Stalin's vicious henchman, he aided the Soviet war effort and development of nuclear weapons.

Beria was facing execution when Sergei Kirov, a Bolshevik commander, decided to spare his life. He would never choose the wrong side again. Millions would come to rue Kirov's mercy, not least the Georgian Mensheviks.

In 1924 Beria gleefully organized the systematic eradication of his previous allies. He would go on to become Joseph Stalin's vicious bloodhound, a lover of torture who was feared even within the corridors of Soviet power.

Lavrentiy Beria was born into a landowning family in Abkhazia (currently a disputed territory of Georgia) on March 29, 1899. After initially supporting the Bolsheviks in 1917, he saw greater opportunities working locally for their enemies: the governing Musavat Party of Azerbaijan and the Mensheviks who controlled Georgia. After the creation of

the Soviet Union in 1922, his "conversion" back to the Bolshevik cause saw him become local deputy head of the OGPU (Joint State Political Directorate), the secret police. He would run advanced spy networks throughout his career.

**Above:** Interior view of a prisoner's room in 1936–7; Beria was responsible for the deaths of hundreds of thousands of Stalin's perceived opponents.
**Opposite:** Lavrentiy Beria with Stalin's daughter Svetlana, with Stalin in the background. The treacherous Beria later claimed that he murdered Stalin.

Beria was put in charge of repressing the anti-Soviet Georgian nationalists, his former allies. Up to 10,000 Georgians were executed in a mass extermination and many more were imprisoned, with Beria personally taking part in torture sessions. The young psychopath had found his sadistic forte, once saying about a prisoner: "Let me have one night with him and I'll have him confessing he's the king of England." Beria was never burdened by a moral imperative to seek the truth. He wanted to inflict such extraordinary pain that a victim would confess to anything.

## STALIN'S ALLY

Beria became head of the Georgian OGPU and in 1926 was introduced to Joseph Stalin, his fellow Georgian, who had begun to take control of the Soviet Union in 1924. Stalin would progressively exterminate all opposition, whether real or imagined. In Lavrentiy Beria, he saw a willing subaltern who would execute his will without the constraints of squeamishness or morality.

Nikita Khrushchev, who would succeed Stalin as leader of the Soviet Union, was soon wary of the leader's new ally: "At first I liked him . . . but gradually his political complexion came clearly into focus. I was shocked by his sinister, two-faced, scheming hypocrisy." Beria's inability to make a long-term friend of Khrushchev would eventually lead to his own death.

By 1932, Beria had become secretary of the Communist Party for Transcaucasia, covering Georgia, Azerbaijan, and Armenia. Like Stalin himself, he was always alert to possible rivals or foes and, in 1936, he plotted against Grigory Ordzhonikidze, a Georgian member of Stalin's Politburo. Ordzhonikidze had grown to dislike Beria and warned Stalin that he was not to be

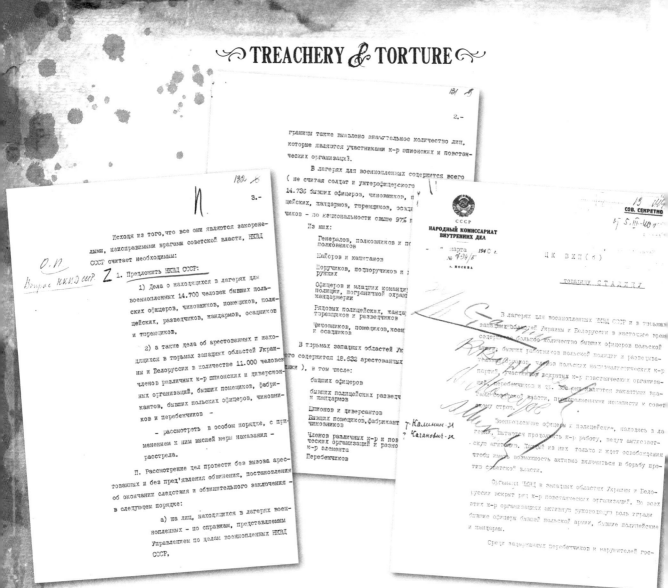

**Above:** Lavrentiy Beria's proposal, signed by Joseph Stalin, for the NKVD U.S.S.R. to exterminate Polish officers, which led to the Katyn Massacre of 1940.

trusted, but Stalin preferred to listen to Beria's counter-whispers. In 1937, Ordzhonikidze died—officially as a result of a heart attack, although it is widely believed that he was assassinated on Stalin's orders.

In 1938, Nikolai Yezkov, the head of the People's

Commissariat for Internal Affairs (the NKVD—effectively the predecessor of the KGB security agency) who had conducted Stalin's Great Purge of opposition in 1936, asked Stalin to appoint Georgy Malenkov as his deputy, only for Stalin instead to inflict on him the dubious charms of Beria. By November of the same year Beria had usurped Yezkov as head of the NKVD. Beria immediately set up new torture chambers at Sukhanovo, a converted monastery, where he would personally oversee brutal interrogation sessions. Stalin's favorite bloodhound was now in position, and a new era of carnage and mayhem began.

The first victims were the staff of the NKVD itself. In a false dawn of liberalization, they were blamed for the excesses of the Great Purge and half of the personnel were removed. Nonetheless, a new purge soon began: from 1940 onward, many Red Army officers were executed and thousands more imprisoned.

## ROLE IN KATYN MASSACRE

Also in 1940, after the Soviets had swept west through Poland in the initial stages of the Second World War, Beria terrorized a new cadre of enemies of the Soviet Union. He directed operations against Polish prisoners with the same merciless pleasure he had shown his native Georgians back in 1924: in April–May 1940, 22,000 Poles, including army personnel, priests, lawyers, and doctors, were slaughtered by Beria's NKVD in mass executions known as the Katyn Massacre.

The massacre remains one of the worst war crimes ever committed, but it only improved Beria's prospects: in 1941 he became deputy prime minister. His gruesome mass organizational skills came into play again as he forced hundreds of thousands of prisoners in the gulag labor camps to work on behalf of the Soviet war effort, including the nuclear program. Then, in 1944, he dealt with the ethnic minorities accused of collaboration with the enemy while the Germans had occupied Soviet lands. About a million Tatars, Chechens, Kalmyks, and other minorities were deported to Soviet Central Asia, while over the course of the 1940s millions more were sent to Siberia. Uprooted from their homes to barren lands and harsh climates, these deportees did not survive long—it is estimated that at least 20 percent of deportees died within a year. It was state-sanctioned mass murder.

In 1946 Beria was made a full member of the Politburo in reward for his wartime activities. While on a diplomatic mission to Moscow, the Yugoslavian communist Milovan Djilas met Beria, whom he described as "short . . . somewhat plump, greenish, and pale, and with soft damp hands . . . square-cut mouth and bulging eyes behind his pince-nez." Perhaps in terms of physique, then, he was Stalin's toad rather than his bloodhound. Although married, Beria would later be portrayed as a serial womanizer and rapist.

## AFTER STALIN

After the war, Beria resigned as head of the NKVD, but he played a pivotal role in establishing Soviet control of Eastern Europe in the postwar period. Increasingly, he was also jockeying for position to replace the aging and increasingly hated Stalin, with whom he no longer enjoyed such good relations. When Stalin died of a stroke in March 1953, Beria claimed he "took him out" himself, according to Soviet diplomat and politician Vyacheslav Molotov, but there remains little evidence.

Beria's main ally, Georgy Malenkov, became prime minister, but Beria was the power behind the throne. However, Beria was deeply distrusted by the rest of the political elite, who also despised the overtures he had made to the United States regarding East Germany in an attempt to secure a stable economic future. Khrushchev, who had not trusted Beria for decades, orchestrated a coup and had him tried as a traitor.

Beria's executioner, General Pavel Batitsky, allegedly had to gag him with a rag to stop his mewling before shooting him in the forehead on December 23, 1953. Khrushchev became the leader of the Soviet Union and denounced the excesses of both Stalin and Beria. ✿

# SAINTS & SINNERS

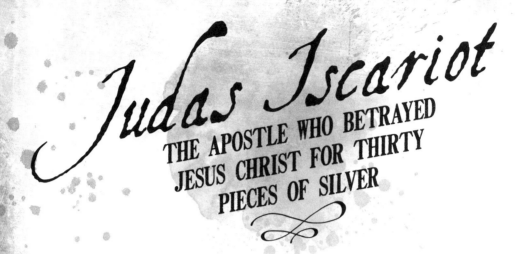

# Judas Iscariot
## THE APOSTLE WHO BETRAYED JESUS CHRIST FOR THIRTY PIECES OF SILVER

The name Judas is synonymous with "betrayer" in many languages of the world. In Christian terms, Judas Iscariot undertook the greatest possible act of treachery: he revealed the whereabouts of Jesus Christ to the authorities, which led to Jesus's crucifixion and death.

There is no contemporary non-biblical historical reference to the figure of Judas Iscariot—and he does not emerge in biblical narratives until the Gospel of St. Mark, believed to have been written c. AD 65–70. All knowledge of Judas's background must be divined from traces of information in the Gospels and the Acts of the Apostles, with the Gospel of St. John providing the greatest detail.

The name Judas is the Greek rendering of the Hebrew Judah,

**Opposite:** A fifteenth-century engraving of Judas Iscariot betraying Jesus Christ by pointing him out to his enemies with a kiss.

which means "God be praised." His surname, Iscariot, suggests that he was from Carioth/Kerioth in Judea. His surname marks a distinction: the rest of the apostles were Galileans, making Judas the Judean an outsider. However, a detail supplied by John, that Judas was "the son of Simon Iscariot," may imply that Judas's father was the newcomer to the region and that Judas grew up locally.

Throughout the Gospels, references to Judas mention his future betrayal. In John's Gospel, Christ's awareness of the role an apostle will play in his death is indicated from the outset: "Jesus answered them: Have not I chosen you twelve; and one of you is a devil? Now he meant Judas Iscariot, the son of Simon: for this same was about to betray him whereas he was one of the twelve."

## MOTIVATED BY MONEY?

There are several references to Judas's role among the apostles: he was the purse carrier, which initiates

### ⸙ FACT FILE ⸙

**Born:** Unknown.
**Died:** c. AD 30–35.
**Historic Feat:** Betrayed Jesus Christ, leading to his crucifixion.
**Circumstances of Death:** Committed suicide by hanging.
**Legacy:** In Christian theology, the traitor whose actions killed Christ, which in turn led to the redemption of humankind.

At the Last Supper, Jesus reveals to Peter which of the apostles will betray him: "He it is to whom I shall reach bread dipped. And when he had dipped the bread, he gave it to Judas Iscariot, the son of Simon. And after the morsel, Satan entered into him. And Jesus said to him: That which thou dost, do quickly." According to Matthew, Judas then became aware of his fate and asked about the betrayer: "Is it I, Rabbi?" and was answered, "Thou hast said it."

## BETRAYAL IN GETHSEMANE

Judas is aware that the Jewish chief priests want Jesus, the strange prophet and troublemaker, imprisoned. He offers to betray Jesus for a reward, which Matthew states is thirty pieces of silver. The traitor then leads a group of armed soldiers and the high priest's servants to Jesus, who has gone by night with the other disciples to the Garden of Gethsemane in Jerusalem, and indicates who he is by kissing him. To this Jesus responds, according to Luke, "Judas, dost thou betray the Son of Man with a kiss?" This initiates the series of events that, according to Christian faith, leads to the crucifixion and resurrection of Christ to save humankind.

The figure of Judas then disappears in three of the Gospels, but Matthew tells of the traitor's repentance, attempt to return the money, and suicide by hanging. However, St. Peter reveals other gory details, in a speech or sermon he gave to his fellow believers that is reported in the Acts of the Apostles 1:16–21. Peter explains that Judas bought a field with the money: "and being hanged, burst asunder in the midst: and all his bowels gushed out. And it became known to all the inhabitants of Jerusalem: so that the same field was called in their tongue, Haceldama, that is to say, the field of blood."

The early Christian bishop Papias of Hierapolis gives a

a link to the greed that will feature in the betrayal. Again, John is the most explicit, saying that Judas, "because he is a thief, and having the purse," protests about the cost of perfume used by Mary of Bethany to anoint Jesus's feet—the money spent could have been used for the poor. Avarice is the motivation given for Judas's betrayal of his master.

**Above:** Saint Mary Magdalene embraces the cross and the feet of Christ at the crucifixion.

**Opposite:** *The Last Supper* (1494–98) by Leonardo da Vinci.

different account, which nonetheless results in a similarly sticky end: "Judas walked about in this world a sad example of impiety; for his body having swollen to such an extent that he could not pass where a chariot could pass easily, he was crushed by the chariot, so that his bowels gushed out."

## THE EFFECT OF HIS ACTIONS

Even though he bears the reputation as the worst traitor ever known, to some, especially the early Christian Gnostics (who wrote an alternative Gospel of Judas in the second century), Judas should be praised: without his betrayal, Christ would not have been crucified and therefore humankind could not have been saved by Christ's sacrifice. To some, Judas's action was preordained, prescribed by fate. Such fatalism or predeterminism is perhaps at odds with the Christian message of self-determinism: that one can choose to save oneself through one's actions. However, to the majority of Christian theologians Judas must bear the full weight of responsibility for the betrayal: Christ's instruction to Judas, "That which thou dost, do quickly," did not predetermine the act; it merely revealed the power of Christ's omniscience.

Whatever the level of self-determinism in the fulfillment of prophesy, the figure of Judas has remained symbolic of utter treachery. In paintings of the Last Supper shared by Christ and the disciples, Judas is depicted as the only apostle with a black halo or without a halo, while the name of the Judas tree (*Cercis siliquastrum*) is linked to the traitor's suicide. ✠

# Nero

## THE FIRST-CENTURY ROMAN EMPEROR WHO USED CHRISTIANS AS HUMAN TORCHES

The Emperor Nero looked over the illuminated gardens with satisfaction. Rome may have burned in a catastrophic fire, but he had managed to lay the blame at the feet of the strange religious zealots whom everyone distrusted: the Christians, who were increasingly practicing their peculiar new cult in Rome. And he had found the perfect punishment, too, for it was those self-same Christians who now illuminated the night sky. Following their arrest, they had been shrouded in wrappers, bound onto posts, and torched.

Nero, who ruled the Roman Empire in AD 54–68, has gone down in history as second only to his uncle Caligula as the most disturbed, cruel, and vengeful of all the Roman

**Opposite:** Nero, the Emperor of Rome who rivaled Caligula in his cruelty and depravity.

## FACT FILE

**Born:** December 15, AD 37, Antium.
**Died:** June 9, AD 68, near Rome.
**Historic Feat:** Extended the Roman Empire and rebuilt Rome after the Great Fire.
**Circumstances of Death:** Committed suicide when Rome turned against him and he faced certain death.
**Legacy:** Known for debauchery, vice, and murder, including those of his wives and mother.

emperors, although both their lives have been subject to wild conjecture. Some Roman historians deemed Nero personally responsible for the Great Fire of Rome, but there is unlikely to be any truth in this. However, he was indubitably capable of monstrous vice. Claims that he murdered some of his own family members, including his mother, and his infamous persecution of the Christians are revealed in terrifying detail in contemporary annals.

## POWERFUL MOTHER

Lucius Domitius Ahenobarbus, who would later take the name Nero, was born into a highly aristocratic Roman family in AD 37. His father Gnaeus was described by the scandal-mongering historian Suetonius as an incestuous, murdering cheat, but he passed away when Lucius was two. The boy's mother, Julia Agrippina, was even more disreputable. The

sister of Caligula, she was deeply entrenched in the political intrigue of Rome and appeared to relish playing power games. She was also suspected of poisoning her second husband. In a tale perverse even by Roman standards, Agrippina then married the Emperor Claudius, her own uncle. She cajoled the emperor into adopting Lucius, who consequently took the name Nero Claudius Caesar. Agrippina then encouraged Nero to marry Octavia, who was Claudius's daughter and thereby both his adoptive sister and his cousin. With Nero now in prime position as the heir to the Roman Empire, it is often contended that his ruthless mother undertook the coup de grâce and murdered Claudius in AD 54.

Nero was just 16 years old when he became the head of the burgeoning empire—young enough for Agrippina to think that she could manipulate the seemingly fey boy, who regarded himself as a poet and art connoisseur. However, the young emperor often preferred to take the sage advice of the philosopher Seneca. In time Nero would show signs of being a capable administrator and was responsible for much building work in Rome, but he was ingrained with his family's murderous streak and a love of vice.

A year after coming to power, it is likely that Nero murdered Claudius's natural son, Britannicus, to ensure that the 14-year-old did not emerge as his imperial rival. His love of debauchery emulated that of his uncle Caligula and there are claims that he had sex with his own mother. Whether due to guilt or a desire to be free of her overbearing influence, Nero had Agrippina killed in AD 59. Octavia, his wife, sister, and cousin, who had always been Agrippina's ally, was dispatched three years later. Meanwhile, the influence of Seneca, Nero's wise mentor, diminished.

Amongst the intrigue and carnage, Nero nevertheless

pursued successful military campaigns, especially in the outreaches of the empire. His generals quelled the Parthian Empire in AD 58–63, Queen Boudicca and the rebellious Iceni were beaten in Britain in AD 61, and the Bosporan kingdom was incorporated into the Roman Empire in AD 63. The following year, Nero would face perhaps the greatest challenge of his imperial rule. Bizarrely, the event would give fuel to both his detractors and the positive revisionists of his reputation for millennia to come.

## WHEN NERO FIDDLED

The Great Fire of Rome devastated the city in July AD 64, causing damage across ten different districts and almost completely destroying three of them. The historians Suetonius and Dio Cassius claimed that Nero himself started the fire and entertained himself by dressing in costume, plucking on his lyre, and singing the "Sack of Ilium" while his people suffered in the flames. The phrase that "Nero fiddled while Rome burned" has

passed into common usage—with "fiddle" presumably meaning a lyre rather than a violin as the latter was not invented for another 1,500 years. In contrast, the more reliable historian Tacitus, who was a child in Rome at the time, claimed that Nero was not even in the city but 30 miles (50 km) away in Antium when the fire started and explained that Christians confessed to arson. If they did, it was doubtless under torture; regarded with distrust by the citizens of Rome, they were a highly suitable scapegoat for Nero.

Christian persecution followed. They were thrown to dogs or crucified, and, according to Tacitus, turned into a spectacle of human torches that lit the emperor's gardens.

**Opposite:** A marble head of Nero.
**Above:** An etching of Nero looking at a tortured woman, while his servants boil oil to continue her ordeal.

Some Christian texts claimed that St. Peter was executed in Rome around this time; he was crucified upside down.

Nero turned the catastrophe to his advantage. Immediately on his return to Rome, he used his own funds to help provide food and shelter for the homeless. In the longer term, he drew up new plans for the wrecked city: he cleared the disreputable, filthy slums, and initiated an extensive series of public works. He also built a flamboyant new villa, the Domus Aurea ("the Golden House"), for himself in the heart of the city. The massive Domus had 300 rooms featuring bejeweled stucco ceilings, frescoes, and white marble.

## EARLY CHRISTIAN MARTYRS

AFTER the crucifixion of Christ around AD 32, the Christian faith spread from the Middle East to Italy during the first century, where it became an underground cult persecuted by the Romans. The Emperor Nero reveled in the hounding of Christians, who were thought to be a threat to Roman society, and had them crucified, torched, and fed to wild dogs. Vitalis, a wealthy convert from Milan, kept his conversion secret but revealed himself when he implored St. Ursicinus to be true to his beliefs when he was threatened with execution. The Roman judge Paulinus ordered the torture of Vitalis on the rack. After enduring horrendous pain but refusing to renounce his faith, Vitalis was buried alive.

## GATHERING OPPOSITION

The administrative capabilities and generosity Nero revealed in the aftermath of the fire would amount to his swansong. Hatred had already set in amongst the political and aristocratic elite of Rome. In AD 65 the pro-Republican statesman Gaius Calpurnius Piso, disgusted by the excesses of the emperor, led an assassination plot that had wide-ranging support. The plot was foiled; nineteen conspirators were executed, thirteen more were exiled, and Piso was forced to commit suicide. By then, Nero was mentally unbalanced and wildly suspicious, and he even forced Seneca to commit suicide. That summer, the emperor killed his second wife, Poppaea Sabina, by kicking her in the abdomen while she was pregnant.

By AD 68, the governor of Gaul was in open revolt, the legions in Germany were discontent, and Galba, the governor of Spain, was firmly opposed to Nero. An emperor who could not control his empire was sure to meet his demise. The prefect of the powerful and ever-fickle Praetorian Guard, the household troops of Rome, turned against Nero in preference for Galba. The Senate declared Nero to be a public enemy and intended to have him beaten to death, but by then Nero had already fled Rome.

On June 9, AD 68, Nero, one of the cruelest emperors known to history, took his own life; it was the anniversary of Octavia's death, so perhaps he regretted at least one of his many murders. He was succeeded by the more level-headed Galba, but he, too, proved unpopular and was assassinated eight months later. ✦

**Opposite:** *The Crucifixion of Saint Peter* by Caravaggio, depicting the upside-down crucifixion of the apostle during Nero's victimization of Christians in Rome, AD 64.

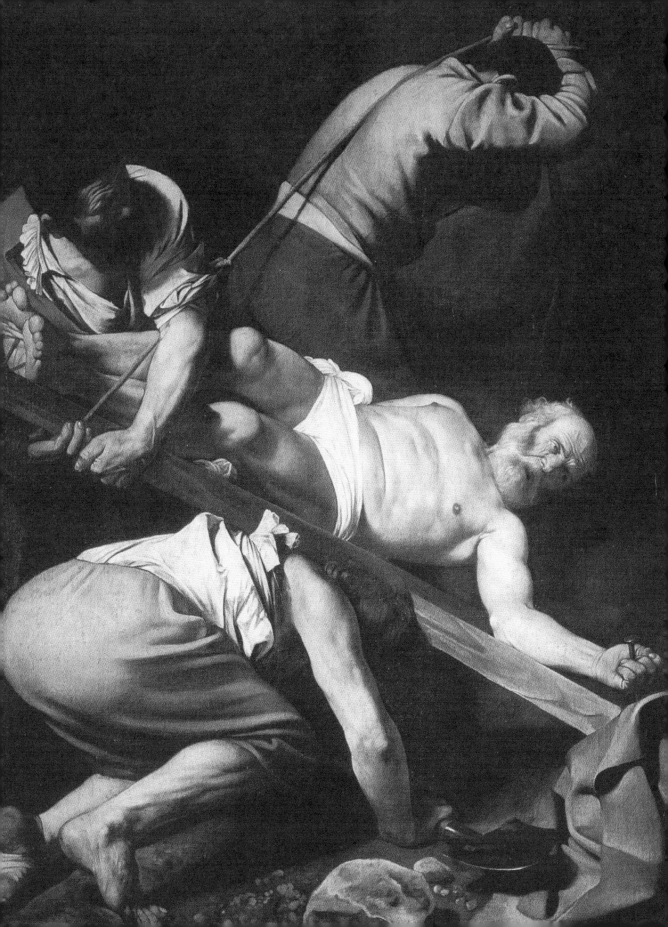

# Joan of Arc

## THE FRENCH GIRL-WARRIOR WHO HEARD THE VOICES OF ANGELS BUT WAS EXECUTED BY BISHOPS

The peasant girl stood in front of the dauphin, but she was not nervous. La Pucelle ("the Virgin" or "Maiden," as she called herself) had walked for eleven days through enemy territory. She was dressed as a boy for the sake of her modesty and to spare her from being raped if she were caught. Now she stood before the dauphin Charles, knowing that she alone had the power to make him king—the angels had told her as much. She would be lauded as the savior of France and the vassal of God. Yet in two years' time, having been found guilty of heresy, she would be tied to a pillar and would feel the scorching heat as the flames beneath her took hold. In the meantime, her words would change history.

Joan of Arc was born in

**Opposite:** Saint Joan of Arc, painted by J. Anthony in 1898, was tried by the Burgundians for heresy and witchcraft.

Domrémy, north-east France, around January 1412. The future of France was hanging in the balance as the Hundred Years' War neared its conclusion. The English kings had been attempting to pursue their claim on French lands for more than ninety years by the time Joan was born, and in 1415 Henry V of England and his esteemed archers destroyed the French army at Agincourt. The victory resulted in the English controlling much of northern France and Henry's son, the future Henry VI, became the heir to the French kingdom. The prospects for the French monarchy were bleak since it also had to contend with enemies even closer to home—the Burgundians—who allied with the English in 1420. Little did Charles, the dauphin and would-be king, know that his fate lay in the hands of a young, illiterate farm-girl who had spent her childhood tending flocks and spinning wool. She

## ⟡ FACT FILE ⟡

**Born:** January 6, c. 1412, Domrémy.
**Died:** May 30, 1431, Rouen.
**Historic Feat:** Helped the French win the Hundred Years' War against the English.
**Circumstances of Death:** Burned to death after being tried for heresy.
**Legacy:** Patron saint and savior of France.

commander, Robert de Baudricourt, to provide an armed escort through enemy territory so that she could have an audience with the dauphin. Initially, de Baudricourt had little time for the messianic ravings of a young shepherdess, but he complied after she accurately predicted yet another defeat for Charles's supporters near Orléans in February 1429. Consequently, Joan and her escort commenced the long walk to Chinon, where Charles had temporarily set up his government. Paris, meanwhile, was in enemy hands, and Reims, where by convention Charles had to be crowned in order to become the king of France, was likewise outside his control.

The dauphin's desperation is apparent in the fact that he granted the fervent, cross-dressed shepherdess an audience at all. He was running out of funds and losing territory, while his remaining armies consisted of untrustworthy mercenaries and ramshackle bands of untrained locals. Meanwhile, English reinforcements were flooding toward the Loire and if Orléans fell, so would all of France. According to an eyewitness, Joan presented herself with "great humility and simplicity," but stated that she was "sent in the name of God to bring aid to yourself and to the kingdom." Charles may have smirked, but then the bizarre virgin-warrior revealed details of a private prayer he had uttered, in which he had questioned his own legitimate right to the throne.

Charles sent Joan to Poitiers to be tested by theologians, who were swayed by her devoutness. While there, in March 1429, she conducted her first onslaught on the English in the form of a dictated letter informing them that the "king of heaven" supported Charles and telling them to "go away to England" or she would expel them. Unsurprisingly, the English took little heed and merely imprisoned her messengers. Greater force would be required.

would become one of the most famous saints—and the most famous female military leader—in history.

## DIVINE GUIDANCE

At the age of 12, Joan started to have visions and hear the voices of angels and saints, but their rather undramatic instructions were merely for her to be "good" and to "go to church regularly." Then, in 1428, just as the English were preparing to take the vital city of Orléans on the River Loire, the angelic messages took on a more specific intent: "Go to France." At that time, the word France would have alluded specifically to the dwindling royal domain controlled by the dauphin Charles. She was told to drive out the English and Burgundians and save Orléans because God supported Charles's claim to the throne.

Joan made three attempts to convince the local

## SIEGE OF ORLÉANS

Joan shaved off her hair and had a suit of armor fitted to her small frame, and was allowed to join the French force at Blois, 30 miles (50 km) from Orléans. This unlikely military strategist was to have an immediate effect on morale. She rallied the beleaguered and discontented soldiers with her fervor and banned prostitutes from the camp. She single-handedly managed to turn a century-old royal conflict into a religious war and reportedly led the army under a banner featuring an image of "Our Savior." Whereas Charles's supporters had previously been filtering away in despondency, now many more men volunteered to fight for the visionary. Her relief force marched from Blois to Orléans. There, the virgin-warrior succeeded where Charles's experienced military campaigners had failed, and she relieved the city from a sustained English siege in May 1429.

Next, she fought the English at Patay, revealing her acute military acumen by suddenly attacking before the English had time to get their lethal archers into position. The English incurred losses of up to 2,500 men, while French casualties only amounted to 100. Joan had predicted that the dauphin would be crowned Charles VII in Reims, and in July 1429, just a few months after she had joined the campaign, he became king of France.

The fortunes of the unlikely military genius soon faltered—and indeed, she had already predicted it would—when she was wounded in the leg by a crossbow and

**Above:** *The Last Communion of Joan of Arc* by Charles-Henri Michel, 1899.
**Opposite:** A model in the guise of Joan of Arc, photographed by Frères Neurdein (Paris), although Joan had severely cropped hair.

failed to capture Paris in September, but she had already turned the war in Charles's favor. Then, in May 1430, she was captured by the Burgundians while campaigning in Compiègne and they sold her to their English allies.

## CONDEMNED AS A WITCH

To the French, Joan was a living saint; to modern medical science, she would perhaps be diagnosed as suffering from a delusional personality disorder; but to the aggrieved English, she was satanic. They imprisoned Joan for a year and then a Burgundian church tribunal—led by an ally of the English, Bishop Pierre Cauchon—concocted claims of heresy and witchcraft.

Joan of Arc was tied to a pillar in Rouen on May 30, 1431, and burned to death. The English burned her

### DEATH BY BURNING

BURNING people to death, usually at the stake, was a favorite method of dispatch in the Middle Ages, particularly for witches and heretics because the accusers wanted the flames to burn away their evil spirits. It is rarely the burning of the flesh—thermal decomposition—that leads to death: in mass burnings, the victims are likely to die from carbon-monoxide poisoning caused by the burning material; in single-person executions, shock and heat-stroke often kill the victim before the fire reaches the vital organs. Approximately 50,000 people were executed as witches and heretics in Europe, primarily in the sixteenth and seventeenth centuries.

corpse twice more to prevent the collection of relics. She was not yet 20 years old. Her death came too late for the English: her victories had damaged their position beyond repair and, before long, the Burgundians switched sides. In time, the English were forced to commence a slow withdrawal from France, bringing the Hundred Years' War to an end. Joan was later canonized by the Catholic Church and remains the patron saint of France. ✣

**Above:** Detail of the Statue of Saint Joan of Arc in Paris.
**Opposite:** Joan of Arc was burned to death in 1431.

# Tomás de Torquemada

## THE MASTERMIND OF RELIGIOUS PERSECUTION IN THE SPANISH INQUISITION IN THE FIFTEENTH CENTURY

The hands of the victim were tied behind his back. The torture master threw the rope over a girder in the ceiling and his assistant attached the end to a hoop in the wall. The rope was then pulled until the victim was hanging in the air from his arms. The weight of his own body ensured that one of his arms was pulled out of its shoulder socket. He would not confess to a crime he had not committed, so the torturer repeatedly let the rope run through his hands and then hauled it down again. The victim twisted and jerked up and down. He screamed and begged for mercy, but still he did not confess.

The robed and tonsured Dominican friar, standing quietly in the corner and watching proceedings, touched the crucifix around his neck and nodded to the torturer. The sweating man and his assistant then tied heavy weights to the victim's ankles. The rope was pulled once more and the victim's other arm popped out of its socket. Finally, the torturer took a pair of metal pincers out of a brazier and applied them to the victim's genitals. The delirious victim started to confess, saying that he was a heretic who had only pretended to convert to the Christian faith. The friar smiled. The inquisition, and the *strappado* torture technique, had rooted out the devil once more.

The friar was Tomás de Torquemada, the leader of the Spanish Inquisition, who would be responsible for the deaths of more than 2,000 Jews and Muslims—and many more yet were tortured. The most infamous monk in history never flinched from performing what he regarded as his holy duty.

Torquemada, born in Valladolid in 1420, was the confessor and confidant of Queen Isabella of Castile, whom he advised to marry King Ferdinand of Aragon. Spain was united under Ferdinand and Isabella's joint rule in 1479. The Iberian peninsula was an

## FACT FILE

**Born:** 1420, Valladolid.

**Died:** September 16, 1498, Ávila.

**Historic Feat:** Masterminded the Spanish Inquisition, the execution of 2,000 Jews and the expulsion of 200,000.

**Circumstances of Death:** Natural causes.

**Legacy:** Responsible for religious persecution and genocide.

insecure territory following hundreds of years of Muslim control, during which many Jews came to the area. The Catholics may have regained control of most of Spain, but they were wary of the Jewish converts they called *marranos* ("pigs"), who had gained increasing political and financial influence. Jews had been forced to convert to Catholicism in order to enjoy full legal rights and protect themselves from violence, but Torquemada suspected that many of the conversions were sham.

## GRAND INQUISITOR, SCOURGE OF HERESY

The Dominican friar convinced Isabella to set up the Tribunal of the Holy Office of the Inquisition into the faith of the converts in 1478, and the enterprise was blessed by Pope Sixtus IV. Despite the use of torture and executions, the Inquisition was initially ineffective, so in 1483 Torquemada took personal control of proceedings under the title of Grand Inquisitor. The persecution of Jewish converts entered a new administrative phase, terrifying in its relentlessness.

The fanatical friar set up a high council and a series of regional tribunals, and insisted that all appeals against the verdicts of the tribunals would go directly to him. They were unlikely to meet with success. Torquemada also laid

**Above:** A priest of the Spanish Inquisition supervises his scribe while victims are suspended from pulleys, tortured on the rack, or burnt with torches.

down twenty-eight articles for his inquisitors to follow in their remit to uncover any vestige of heresy, sorcery, usury, renunciation of the faith, or sodomy. Torture was religiously sanctioned, and the use of *strappado*, the rack, and burning by hot coals became commonplace. Although mutilation was not condoned, it certainly occurred. All acts of torture could be forgiven by a fellow inquisitor.

## REIGN OF TERROR

The Spanish populace was encouraged to help the Inquisition by informing on Jewish neighbors: if two people made an accusation against a convert, an inquiry and, often, torture would follow. If they did not confess, they were imprisoned for life or executed. The condemned had to wear a penitential cloak, some of which were decorated with flames. If accused people died prior to being found guilty, their bodies were dug up and burned.

In the course of Torquemada's Inquisition, about 2,000 heretical converts were burned at the stake or beheaded, and many others died in prison, although some historians give a far higher figure.

## EXPULSION OF THE JEWS

Torquemada was not content with the slaughter of converts: he counseled Isabella and Ferdinand to remove every single Jew from Spain. Following the Alhambra Decree of March 31, 1492, 200,000 Jews were expelled from the region, even though some of their families had been resident in Spain for centuries and their presence

**Above:** Tomás de Torquemada (1420–98), the Spanish Dominican monk and Inquisitor-General.
**Opposite:** Accused heretics standing before a tribunal of the Spanish Inquisition in Seville, depicted by Édouard Moyse in the late nineteenth century.

was highly beneficial for the economy.

Spanish Catholics began to turn against the inquisitors as evidence started to emerge that their zeal and propensity to use torture cost the lives of innocent people, while profit was being made from the confiscation of the condemned people's property. Torquemada himself had to travel with a huge armed guard to protect him from attack. Meanwhile, the new pope, Alexander VI, was dubious of the merits of the Inquisition and put in place measures to rein in the scale of the torture.

However, after Torquemada died on September 16, 1498, the Spanish Inquisition continued. In 1501 the remaining Muslims in Spain were forced to convert or face expulsion, and were subjected to the same persecution as the Jews. A small number of Protestants were also executed in the sixteenth century. The Inquisition, whose birth had been masterminded by this sinister priest, continued episodically right through to 1834. ✛

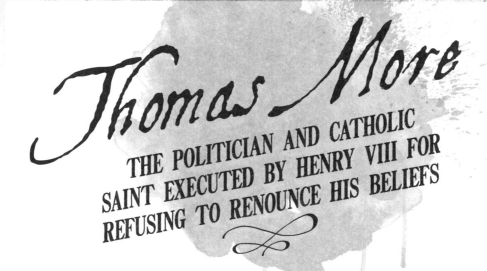

# Thomas More

## THE POLITICIAN AND CATHOLIC SAINT EXECUTED BY HENRY VIII FOR REFUSING TO RENOUNCE HIS BELIEFS

Thomas More sat alone at a writing table in the Tower of London and considered his life. He had been many things—lawyer, historian, theologian, and, not least, Henry VIII's chancellor, which had made him the second most powerful man in England—but one thing he had never been was a coward. The king had given him an ultimatum, and More could save himself with one dip of the quill in the ink. The tip of his quill remained white and pure. Thomas More had chosen death.

More was born in London on February 7, 1478. He was a devout Catholic and considered becoming a priest, but instead chose to follow his father into the law. Recognized as hugely intelligent, witty, and

**Opposite:** Thomas More by Hans Holbein the Younger.

### ❧ FACT FILE ❧

**Born:** February 7, 1478, London.
**Died:** July 6, 1535, London.
**Historic Feat:** Henry VIII's Lord Chancellor who refused to betray his Catholic faith.
**Circumstances of Death:** Beheaded, having been spared the ignominy of being hanged, drawn, and quartered.
**Legacy:** One of England's greatest thinkers, who was made a Catholic saint in 1935.

honorable, he became an undersheriff of London in 1510, and entered the service of King Henry VIII seven years later. Henry was known as a great sportsman and lover of hunting, but he also had a deep interest in philosophy, and in More he had found one of the greatest minds of the kingdom. More worked as his secretary and soon became his most trusted diplomatic aide. He was rewarded with a knighthood in 1521.

Simultaneously, More continued his scholarly work. In 1515, he wrote his *History of King Richard III*, which to this day is considered a great early example of the art of historiography, despite its somewhat biased characterization of the king: the casting of Richard as a tyrant no doubt appealed to More's master, the king, since it was Henry's own father, Henry VII, who had wrested the crown from Richard and created the Tudor dynasty. A year later,

in 1516, More completed his greatest work, *Utopia*, in which he depicted a fictional island in the Atlantic. In contrast to the muddled morality of the often warring European kingdoms, his Utopia was a perfect and ethically responsible state.

## RELIGIOUS REFORM

More was an admirer of Erasmus of Rotterdam, a radical theologian and humanist who called for reform of the

**Above:** Portrait of King Henry VIII, a copy of a lost work by Hans Holbein the Younger. Henry eventually executed More, his former Chancellor and ally.
**Opposite:** An illustration of More's imaginary Utopia from the first edition of the work, 1516.

Catholic Church, and his interest was soon shared by Henry. Like Erasmus, More believed that the Catholic Church needed to evolve but he rejected Lutheran Protestantism and its emphasis on personal faith alone, free of the constraints of the established Church.

More was a staunch supporter of the Catholic faith and the papacy. He wrote pamphlets on the dangers of heresy, and he helped to ban Protestant Reformist tracts he considered to be heretical. After he was appointed Lord Chancellor by Henry in 1529, he interrogated those who turned against orthodox religion. The sixteenth-century writer John Foxe accused More of personally torturing and whipping Protestant heretics. Six heretics were burned at the stake, including clergymen, a lawyer, and John Tewkesbury, a leatherseller who had been arrested for possession of banned books. More felt little remorse for the executions, writing that Tewkesbury "burned as there was neuer wretche I wene better worthy." However, More soon came to realize that the most wretched "heretic" was his own friend and master.

## THE KING'S DIVORCE

Henry wished to divorce Catherine of Aragon, primarily because she had not borne him a male heir, but needed the consent of the pope in Rome. More's predecessor as chancellor, Cardinal Thomas Wolsey, had failed in this endeavor and faced trial by treason as a consequence. More supported the king's right to divorce as he shared scholarly opinion that the marriage had been unlawful from the outset. However, he continued to support the authority of the pope over the king of England. In 1532, after Henry made it clear that he would split the English Church from Rome and declare himself to be the supreme head of the Church in England, More resigned as Lord Chancellor. He refused to take an oath declaring that the king was the head of the Church, and similarly refused to acknowledge the annulment of the king's first marriage. He effectively stated that Henry's new marriage, to Anne Boleyn, was unlawful before God.

In 1534, Henry arrested More for treason and imprisoned him in the Tower of London. More could have picked up his quill to ask Henry for clemency and agree to take the oath. However, when he did finally dip the feather in the ink, it was to write *A Dialogue of Comfort Against Tribulation*, in which he stated that God was the only comfort in the face of martyrdom.

More's trial was hardly fair: the panel of judges included three of Anne Boleyn's close family. He refused to speak, knowing that if he did not explicitly state that

Henry was not the supreme head of the Church he could not be convicted. However, the court simply brought in a witness to claim, almost undoubtedly falsely, that More had said those very words. More was destined to become one of the greatest martyrs in English history.

Just prior to his execution by beheading on July 6, 1535, More said, "I die the king's good servant, but God's first." Ever the wit, he said to the executioner that his beard had committed no crime and did not deserve the ax, and positioned himself so it would not be sliced by the blade. More is esteemed as one of England's greatest philosophical scholars and was canonized as a Catholic saint, an event unlikely to befall many other politicians. ✠

# René Goupil

## THE FIRST AMERICAN SAINT, WHO WAS TORTURED AND MARTYRED BY NATIVE AMERICANS IN THE SEVENTEENTH CENTURY

When René Goupil was forced to leave the Jesuit novitiate and give up his training to become a monk, he must have thought he would never be able to fulfill his intention to live as a servant of Christ. Just a couple of years afterward, however, he would become the first Christian martyr in North America, and almost 300 years later he would be canonized as the first American saint.

Goupil was born in Saint-Martin-du-Bois in Anjou, France, in 1608 and was baptized on May 15 of that year. He briefly worked as a surgeon in Orléans before he joined the Jesuit novitiate in Paris in 1639. Illness and deafness prevented him from completing his training to become a novice and join the Jesuit religious order.

Despite the setback, Goupil volunteered to help the Jesuits who had traveled to Quebec in New France, North America, both to serve the new colonist settlers and to convert the native population. From 1640, he put his medical skills to good use by tending to the sick in the hospital of the Saint Joseph de Sillery Jesuit mission. Two years later, he joined a party of forty, led by Father Isaac Jogues, to travel by canoe to the Jesuits' Sainte-Marie mission settlement in Huron territory. The group, which included members of the Huron people, was captured by warriors of the Mohawk Iroquois near Lake St. Peter. The missionaries were regarded as legitimate targets by the Iroquois because of their association with the Huron, with whom they had been fighting a sustained war. The missionaries and early European settlers were further demonized due to the foreign diseases such as smallpox that they had unwittingly introduced to native populations in the seventeenth century.

## ☙ FACT FILE ❧

**Born:** May 1608, Saint-Martin-du-Bois.

**Died:** September 29, 1642, Ossernenon.

**Historic Feat:** A Jesuit missionary who died at the hands of the Mohawk Iroquois tribe.

**Circumstances of Death:** Executed with a tomahawk.

**Legacy:** The first U.S. Catholic saint who is one of the collective North American Martyrs.

## BRUTAL ATTACK

The missionaries underwent torture, including beatings, and René Goupil had his nails ripped from his fingers and then the ends of some of his fingers cut off. On the thirteen-day journey to the Iroquois territory of Ossernenon (modern-day Auriesville in New York State), he endured heat stroke and festering wounds, and was beaten almost to death. On arrival at Ossernenon, he and Father Jogues had to survive further torture and punishment. Goupil professed vows in the presence of Father Jogues and became a Jesuit lay brother. He consequently attempted to teach Iroquois children the sign of the cross. As a result, on September 29, 1642, he was killed by several blows to the head with a tomahawk. Father Isaac Jogues,

who survived the ordeal at the hands of the Native Americans, described Goupil in a letter as "an angel of innocence and a martyr of Jesus Christ."

Father Jogues, who was from Orléans, also had two fingers cut off, and he had to endure a further year as a slave of the Iroquois. He was a strong and resolute figure, known to the Mohawks as "Ondessonk" or "the indomitable one," who had been a missionary working among the native peoples since 1636. Dutch traders eventually bought his freedom from the Iroquois, just before he was due to be burned to death. He went by

**Above:** An engraving based on Samuel de Champlain's drawing of a battle between Iroquois and Algonquian tribes.

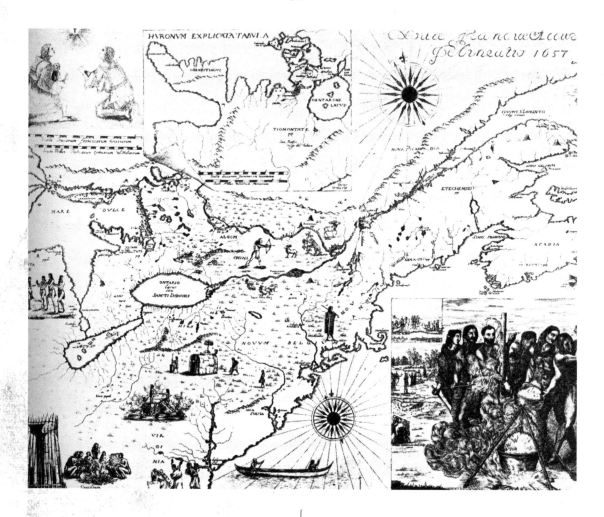

boat to New York (still known as New Amsterdam at the time) and became the first Christian missionary to set foot on Manhattan island. He returned to France but, despite his previous horrendous experiences, returned to North America within a few months to continue his missionary work.

In 1646, he and a 19-year-old Jesuit layman called Jean de Lalande were sent to Iroquois territory as ambassadors after a tentative peace had been forged between the French, the Huron, and the Iroquois. However, the Mohawks blamed Father Jogues and

the practice of his religious "sorcery" for the failure of their crops and a spate of illness. He and Lalande were taken prisoner near Lake George, stripped, and slashed with knives. He met a similar fate to René Goupil and was decapitated with a tomahawk at Ossernenon on

**Above:** François-Joseph Bressani's map of 1657 includes a drawing of the Iroquois torture and murder of Jean de Brébeuf and Gabriel Lalemant.
**Opposite:** Statue of Saint Isaac Jogues teaching two Mohawk Indian children, located in the grounds of the National Shrine of the North American Martyrs, Auriesville, New York.

October 18, 1646. Jean de Lalande was executed in the same manner on the following day.

## HONORED BY THE POPE

René Goupil, Father Isaac Jogues, and Jean de Lalande were three of eight executed Jesuit missionaries all associated with the "Sainte-Marie among the Hurons" mission settlement, and are collectively known as the North American Martyrs. The remaining five missionaries—Jean de Brébeuf, Noël Chabanel, Antoine Daniel, Charles Garnier, and Gabriel Lalemant—were all killed by the Iroquois in 1648 and 1649.

The eight martyrs were canonized as Catholic saints by Pope Pius XI in 1930, with René Goupil, the first martyr to die on American soil, becoming the first U.S. saint. The martyrs, all of whom were originally from France, are the secondary patron saints of Canada. Schools in Canada and the United States are named after them, while the National Shrine of the North American Martyrs, also dedicated to Our Lady of Martyrs, is in Auriesville, New York, near the site of the murders of Goupil, Jogues, and Lalande. The Jesuits did eventually have some effect on the Mohawk Iroquois: a Mohawk woman, Kateri Tekakwitha, born in Ossernenon in 1656, also became a Catholic saint. ✛

## SCALPING

NATIVE Americans, colonists, and frontiersmen all practiced scalping during the frontier conflicts in North America from the seventeenth to the nineteenth centuries. Scalping, in which the scalp of a usually deceased victim's head is sliced off (preferably in one piece) with a blade as a battle trophy, had been employed by some Native American tribes since at least the fourteenth century. The colonists copied the practice, and placed a bounty on each Native American scalp. Ranger John Lovewell, whose own parents had been murdered and scalped, famously went on scalp-hunting missions against the Abenaki in the 1720s.

# Rasputin

## THE MAD RUSSIAN MONK WHO ADHERED TO A CULT THAT BELIEVED DOING WRONG WAS GOOD FOR THE SOUL

"**S**in that you may obtain forgiveness." It was a strange mantra for someone who declared himself to be a "holy man," but the entire story of Rasputin, an illiterate peasant who became the mysterious, mystical adviser to the tsarina of Russia, is peculiar, right down to the details of his assassination.

Grigori Yefimovich Novyk, who would become known to the world as Rasputin, was born in Pokrovskoye in remote Siberia in 1869. He was the fifth child of Siberian peasants and had no formal education whatsoever, and only learned to read and write in adulthood. He married at the age of 18 and had three children, but in 1892 he left his village and his family to join an Eastern Orthodox monastery.

**Opposite:** Grigori Yefimovich Novyk, the debauched Russian mystic known as Rasputin, who was rumored to have slept with the tsarina and her older daughters.

### ☙ FACT FILE ❧

**Born:** January 10, 1869, Pokrovskoye.
**Died:** December 17, 1916, St. Petersburg.
**Historic Feat:** Illiterate peasant who became an advisor to the tsar and tsarina of Russia.
**Circumstances of Death:** Poisoned, shot, beaten, and drowned by Russian nobles.
**Legacy:** The Mad Monk's activities increased displeasure with the tsar shortly before the Russian Revolution.

However, a conventional religious life did not appeal to Grigori and by 1900 he had become a mystic, wandering around the country and claiming to have visions.

The "Mad Monk," as he became known, was a tall and peculiarly charismatic man, with long, center-parted hair and an unkempt beard. He had an unusually strong character, a deep, hypnotic voice, and staring eyes, which he used to transfix people. He earned his keep by wandering from town to town, claiming that he could cure the sick through his supernatural powers; he supposedly also made innumerable sexual conquests. Despite his self-portrayal as a holy man with links to the Orthodox Church, Rasputin preached the bizarrely self-serving theology of the Khlysty underground sect, that the more you sinned, the more you were forgiven and the more holy you became. Rasputin enacted his own advice as often as possible.

Even though his name was synonymous with debauchery—his assumed name, Rasputin, means "debauched one"—his healing powers and mysticism attracted the attention of aristocratic circles in St. Petersburg. In 1906, when one of Prime Minister Pyotr Stolypin's children was injured in an assassination attempt, Tsar Nicholas II of Russia called on Rasputin to visit the child.

## ROYAL FAVORITE

In the following year, the tsar requested Rasputin's services again, this time on behalf of his own son, Alexei. The boy, who suffered from hemophilia, had cut himself and the royal doctors had failed to stop the hemorrhage. Tsarina Alexandra, Nicholas's spouse and the granddaughter of Queen Victoria of England, was desperate—and allowed the mysterious mystic to treat her son. Rasputin succeeded where nascent conventional medicine had failed and stopped Alexei's bleeding, possibly through the use of hypnotism.

Grateful and supposedly enraptured by Rasputin, Alexandra allowed the monk to become a fixture at the royal court in St. Petersburg, and his influence spread well beyond the welfare of Alexei. Rasputin pontificated on all manner of subjects as if his opinion was ordained by God, and surprisingly the increasingly beleaguered Nicholas gave credence to his views: he had so little knowledge of the peasantry that he mistook Rasputin as representative of peasants' opinion.

Access to the court extended the spectrum of possibility for Rasputin's debauchery and he indulged in wild parties in which revelers pursued his maxim of sinning to obtain forgiveness. It is alleged that Rasputin added the tsarina herself to his list of conquests, a dubious claim nonetheless given some credence by a telegram she once sent to Rasputin:

"I sacrifice my husband and my heart to you. Pray and bless. Love and kisses—darling."

Prime Minister Stolypin was not so enamored. He suspected that Rasputin was a fraud and initiated an inquiry into the monk's behavior. As a result, Rasputin was removed from the court at St. Petersburg, but the tsarina remained a dedicated follower of the Mad Monk. After Stolypin was assassinated in 1911, Rasputin was allowed to return to the court.

## WIDE-RANGING POWERS

Stolypin was not the only member of the Russian nobility to abhor Rasputin's depravity and political influence, but the tsar and tsarina ignored the detractors. In 1915, during the First World War, the tsar left St. Petersburg to take charge of proceedings at the German front, leaving Alexandra in charge of the country's domestic affairs. She turned to her confidant for assistance and Rasputin began to oversee political and ecclesiastical appointments. He claimed that he had divine insight, but he appointed evidently incompetent people to powerful positions, much to the concern of nobles who feared for the governance of Russia and, less altruistically, for their own futures in the face of a popular uprising.

For well over a decade, displeasure with the remote and often ineffectual tsar had been growing, and the influence of the morally incontinent mystic worsened matters. Rasputin, it was rumored, was also accepting bribes—both monetary and sexual—in exchange for influencing the court. Furthermore, he often appeared to be intoxicated. Some of the more extreme stories about the mystic may have been the work of anti-imperial Bolsheviks, but they had plenty of material with which to work.

Nicholas, meanwhile, was doing little to enhance his reputation by catastrophically mismanaging the war with

Germany. The Russian army was sustaining huge losses. There was also a growing suspicion that the tsarina, who was related to the German kaiser, was a spy conspiring with Rasputin to advance the enemy cause.

## ASSASSINATION PLOT

In December 1916, with support for Bolshevism on the rise, the nobles decided to save Russia by expunging what seemed to be the most easily removable element of the distrusted imperial triumvirate: they plotted to kill Rasputin.

**Above:** The influence of Rasputin initially extended to nobles such as Prince Mikhail Putyatin (left), but he was seen as a dangerous liability as the Russian public turned against Tsar Nicholas.
**Opposite:** The aftermath of an assassination attempt on Prime Minister Pyotr Stolypin on August 12, 1906.

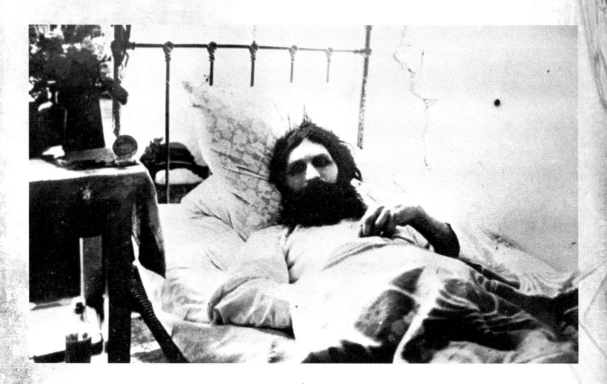

The varied accounts of the almost vaudevillian assassination include some unlikely details, but it seems that first of all the plotters tried to poison Rasputin with cyanide-laced wine and cakes. The mystic consumed enough to kill five men, but suffered no adverse effects. Prince Yusupov, one of the conspirators, then shot him at close range, but when he leaned over to check his seemingly dead body, Rasputin grabbed him and stared at him with his famously hypnotic eyes. The other assassins, who allegedly included British secret service agents, then fired three more bullets into him. When it became apparent that Rasputin had survived this

**Above:** Rasputin recovering in hospital after being stabbed in 1914 by a peasant, Khioniya Goseva, who called him "the Antichrist." He was assassinated in 1916.
**Opposite:** A caricature of Rasputin by N. Ivanov, dating from c. 1910, ridiculing the strange mystic's influence over the tsar and tsarina.

further onslaught of lead, the conspirators went into panic mode and tried to club him to death. Finally, it seemed that the Mad Monk was dead, but nonetheless they bound his body with rope and threw him in the freezing River Neva. The autopsy report revealed that Rasputin had water in his lungs, so despite the attempted poisoning, five bullet wounds, and a sustained beating, he died from drowning.

The death of Rasputin did nothing to save the fortunes of imperial Russia. The populace's hatred for the inept tsar and his tsarina did not subside with the removal of their corrupt advisor. Nicholas, Alexandra, and their children would only survive for eighteen months after Rasputin's death. The 1917 Bolshevik revolutions brought the communists to power and, in July 1918, the whole family was executed. Meanwhile, Rasputin, not least because of the tale of his death, became the most infamous mystic who had ever walked the Earth. ✠

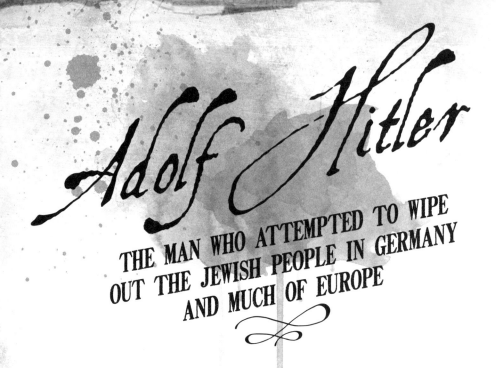

# Adolf Hitler

## THE MAN WHO ATTEMPTED TO WIPE OUT THE JEWISH PEOPLE IN GERMANY AND MUCH OF EUROPE

At 2:30 p.m. the little man, who loved his nation, his dogs, children, music, and art, led the woman he had married just 40 hours earlier into his private study. An hour later, his valet, Heinz Linge, his adjutant Otto Günsche, and his favorite aide, Martin Bormann, heard a gunshot. Opening the study door, the valet was hit by the smell of burnt almonds. Günsche pushed past Linge and saw his boss slumped on the sofa, and later recalled that he was "sunken over, with blood dripping out of his right temple. He had shot himself with his own pistol, a Walther PPK 6.65." Blood was running down his face, soaking into the arm of the sofa, and forming a red puddle on the floor. The reason for the smell of

**Opposite:** Adolf Hitler used his famously powerful oratory skills to infuse mass support for the Nazi Party in the 1920s and 1930s.

### ~❧FACT FILE❧~

**Born:** April 20, 1889, Braunau am Inn.
**Died:** April 30, 1945, Berlin.
**Historic Feat:** Started the Second World War, conquered much of Europe, and unleashed the Holocaust in which 6 million Jews were exterminated.
**Circumstances of Death:** Committed suicide with his wife when he faced capture.
**Legacy:** The most hated dictator in history; it took decades to rebuild Europe after the Second World War.

almonds was immediately apparent. Cyanide had scented the air: the man had bitten down into a capsule and his new bride, Eva, was curled up on the sofa next to him, also lifeless.

The date was April 30, 1945. Adolf Hitler, who had ordered the extermination of 6 million Jews and initiated an ego-driven war of such magnitude and violence that it took the lives of a further 60 million people across the world, had committed suicide rather than face trial and execution.

Hitler was not born in Germany but in Austria on April 20, 1889. He was raised in a working-class German-Austrian family and attended a technical school in Linz, where he failed to excel. Hitler claimed he deliberately did badly at school so his father "would let me devote myself to my dream" – to become an artist. His father died when he was 14, and Hitler moved to Vienna a couple of

years later, initially working as a laborer to finance his nascent artistic career and bohemian lifestyle. At the same time, Hitler had a burgeoning interest in German nationalism and resolutely believed that Austria should be subsumed into the "fatherland."

## RISE TO POWER

After moving to Munich in 1913, Hitler fought as a volunteer in Germany's Bavarian Army in the First World War, winning the Iron Cross. Following Germany's defeat, he became an intelligence agent for the army and spied on the German Workers' Party as an undercover agent. However,

**Above:** Jewish shops and synagogues throughout Germany and Austria were attacked by Brownshirts and Nazi sympathizers on Kristallnacht ("Crystal Night"), also known as the "Night of Broken Glass," on November 9–10, 1938.
**Opposite:** The Nazis boycotted Jewish shops in a campaign of alienation.

Hitler was genuinely attracted to the party's nationalistic and anti-Semitic policies, and in 1921, having left the army, he became the party's leader. Meanwhile, the party had been renamed the *Nationalsozialistische Deutsche Arbeiterpartei* (the National Socialist German Workers' Party, commonly known as the Nazi Party), and Hitler had personally designed its new logo—a black swastika on a white circle with a red background.

Under Hitler's leadership, Nazi policy calcified into zealous right-wing nationalism, anti-Semitism and anti-communism, and the party had a reputation for violence through its Stormtrooper organization, nicknamed the Brownshirts. Hitler led the Nazis in a failed coup in 1923 and served nine months in jail, where he wrote his radical autobiography, *Mein Kampf*.

On his release, his popularity grew rapidly. In an era of social and economic turmoil, his charisma, speechmaking, and racial radicalism were an elixir to a section of the population who wanted national pride to return after the emasculation of Germany in the First World War. Hitler had the power to captivate the public through his potent and intense oratory, and huge crowds would gather in adoration to witness his speeches, delivered with a fervent, almost crazed evangelism. To many, the short man with the toothbrush moustache was the savior of Germany. The Nazi Party exploded in size and Hitler attracted a cadre of supremely loyal henchmen, including Reinhard Heydrich (whom even Hitler called "the man with the iron heart") and Heinrich Himmler, who would help him persecute Germany's racially "impure" elements and make Germany great again.

With the other parties unable to ignore his support, Hitler became chancellor of a coalition government in 1933. The resoluteness of Hitler's rhetoric was matched by the violence of the Nazi Brownshirts, who terrorized opponents with gleeful savagery. Hitler soon announced that the Nazis were the single legal party in Germany, and began the systematic persecution of the Jewish population. He was now the führer, the dictator of Germany, and his unrelenting determination, lust for power, and hatred would bring devastation to the world.

## RUTHLESS EXPANSION

Hitler sought to restore what he regarded as stolen German lands over its borders and pursued the policy of *Lebensraum*—more "living room" for his beloved German people. In March 1936, German troops illegally flooded

into the Rhineland on the border with France. Over the course of the next three years he would annex Austria and Czechoslovakia. France and Britain at first stood by, unwilling to engage in another war following the carnage of 1914–18. Hitler had no such qualms. In September 1939, he invaded Poland and provoked the greatest war in history.

**Above and opposite:** Hitler, responsible for the worst genocide in history, was very affectionate to both dogs and children. He and Eva Braun committed suicide on April 30, 1945, shortly after their wedding.

Hitler had two major advantages compared to his enemies: he was prepared for full-scale war and he was utterly ruthless. By mid-1940, France had been defeated and initial British resistance had failed: the British limped back across the English Channel. Hitler, it seemed, was not only a brutal evangelist but also a master tactician.

In the early years of the war his popularity in Germany soared still further. Older sons were sent willingly into battle to sacrifice their lives for Hitler's Third Reich; younger children showed their devotion to the führer by joining the Nazi Youth. True advocates of Nazism and excellent military leaders were rewarded with honors and privileges, but famously, Hitler could turn on even the most loyal officer, flying into a shouting, spittle-spraying rage. Many Germans became acolytes of his masterplan—no matter how extreme and cruel—through zealous loyalty and fear in equal measure.

Hitler was now free to pursue an extensive policy of ethnic cleansing in German-occupied lands. Millions of Jews, Romanies, and Slavs were exterminated, largely in death camps in German-occupied territory, along with homosexuals and political opponents. Many more were forced to endure slave labor and starvation. They were no longer considered human.

## DECLINE AND FALL

In the end, Hitler's obstinacy was his downfall. He permanently damaged his resources by engaging in an entrenched battle with the Soviet Union in the east, which allowed the British, Americans, and their allies to push through France and Italy from June 1944 onward. Loyalty to Hitler began to waiver in the face of certain defeat, and high-ranking officers mounted several plots to assassinate their führer to put an end to the terrible bloodshed: they knew he would never surrender and, in the meantime, many more German lives were being sacrificed.

By April 1945, the Allies were surrounding Berlin, and Adolf Hitler finally acknowledged that the end was inevitable as he took refuge in his bunker. Obdurate to the last, he preferred death over surrender and humiliation. He married his girlfriend Eva Braun in a small private ceremony and led her into his study in the bunker. After their joint suicide, their remains were burned by his remaining loyal staff shortly before Soviet forces arrived. The genocide conducted by the most callous dictator in history was about to be fully exposed, but he would never face justice for his crimes against humanity. ✠

# Mahatma Gandhi

## THE DEVOUT, PEACE-LOVING INDIAN LEADER WHO WAS ASSASSINATED BY A HINDU EXTREMIST

In 1947, as millions of people took to the streets to celebrate India's independence from Britain, one man who should have been at the very heart of the celebrations sat quietly in contemplation. Mahatma Gandhi, more than any other individual, was responsible for freeing India from the yoke of imperialism, but he sought no glory. He merely worried that the simultaneous division of India into separate Hindu and Muslim countries was a failure that would lead to awful violence. Soon, Gandhi, the greatest figure in Indian political history—the "Father of the Nation"—would be counted among the dead. He remains lauded as a man who never strayed from pacifism or his determination to live by his principles.

Mohandas Karamchand Gandhi was born on October 2, 1869, in Porbandar, India. The country had become an official part of the British Empire in 1858, but had effectively been under British control for a century. Gandhi studied law in London before settling in South Africa, where he practiced as a barrister. His interest in judicial rights extended to attempting to right social ills. While in South Africa, he became a political activist and emerged as a leader of the Indian community there, focused on combating racial discrimination. He was repeatedly arrested and imprisoned for his activities, but the government was forced to cede ground. It was the start of a lifetime's dedication to the pursuance of a non-discriminating society, which would make him the most famous pacifist in history.

## SATYAGRAHA

In 1915, Gandhi returned to India and his political career accelerated. He spearheaded campaigns against the injustices of British rule, notably its excessive taxes and institutionalized racial discrimination. By 1921, he

### ~ FACT FILE ~

**Born:** October 2, 1869, Porbandar.
**Died:** January 30, 1948, Delhi.
**Historic Feat:** Led India toward independence from British rule.
**Circumstances of Death:** Assassinated by Hindu extremist Nathuram Godse.
**Legacy:** The world's most famous pacifist, who preached nonviolence in the face of oppression.

was the head of the Indian National Congress party and advocated the use of nonviolent noncooperation with the British authorities as a weapon for change. The ultimate aim of this policy of *satyagraha*, which roughly means "devotion to truth," was to bring about the demise of British colonialism without resorting to war or violence. Gandhi explained, "An eye for an eye only ends up making the whole world blind." Once again, though, he was regarded as an enemy of the authorities. He was imprisoned for two years from 1922 on charges of sedition.

On his release, he continued to organize campaigns of civil disobedience, hunger strikes, and a boycott of British goods; the British Empire was always a commercial enterprise, and he knew he could strike at its heart with monetarily punitive measures.

In 1930 he organized a mass repudiation of the salt laws, through which Britain monopolized salt production in India, and spearheaded the 250-mile (400-km) "Salt March" protest. Britain was growing weary of the disruptions and Gandhi was invited to discuss the prospect of Indian independence at a conference in London, but it was clear that there would be no progress without further damaging campaigns. He maintained his policy of *satyagraha*, however, and left the Indian National Congress in 1934 in protest against the use of violence.

**Above:** In March–April 1930, Gandhi undertook a 250-mile march in protest against the punitive salt tax imposed by the British administration in India.

## NEHRU-GANDHI ASSASSINATIONS

THE name Gandhi would be associated with Indian politics—and assassinations—long after Mahatma Gandhi's death. Indira Gandhi and her son Rajiv Gandhi both became prime minister of India, and both were assassinated, but they were not related to the Mahatma. Indira was the daughter of Jawaharlal Nehru, who was a follower of Mahatma Gandhi's noncooperation movement and became the first prime minister of India following independence. Indira coincidentally married a man with the surname Gandhi and was prime minister twice. She was murdered by her Sikh bodyguards in 1984. Her son Rajiv succeeded her and was killed by a Tamil suicide bomber—a woman who had explosives hidden under her dress—in 1989.

## "GREAT SOUL"

Rather than indulging himself with the trappings of power, he lived a spartan life from the mid-1930s onward. His home had no running water or electricity; he owned very little; he practiced strict vegetarianism; and he wore a *dhoti*, a single piece of white cloth, wrapped around his body. By this time Gandhi was often referred to as Mahatma (Sanskrit for "Great Soul"). He was a devout but open-minded Hindu who believed that religious and social tolerance was essential to the future of India: he was adamant that Hindus, Muslims, Christians, Sikhs, Buddhists, and Jains could live together in an independent India without conflict.

With independence seemingly no nearer, in 1942 Gandhi asked all Indians to risk their lives in the name of freedom. Mass opposition became rife and Britain, a weak imperial power further weakened by the travails of the Second World War, had no option but to accede to independence in 1947.

## PARTITION

Gandhi's dream of a unified nation and religious harmony was destroyed in the process. Britain, now seeking to extract itself from India at speed, accepted Muslim leaders' calls for a separate Muslim state, and agreed to partition the country. Northern territories were hived off to become the Muslim states of West Pakistan and East Pakistan (the latter is now Bangladesh). Consequently, Gandhi did not celebrate independence; he went on hunger strike in protest at the ensuing violence.

**Opposite (top):** Gandhi fasting in the 1920s, pictured with the young Indira Gandhi (née Nehru), who like her mentor would later be assassinated by extremists.

**Opposite (bottom):** Gandhi's assassin, the Hindu militant Nathuram Godse.

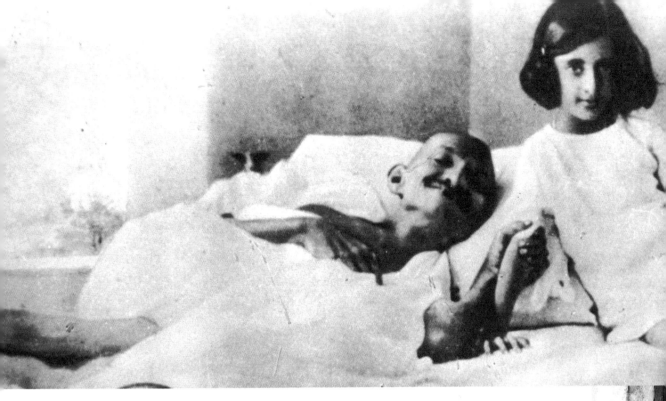

The partition caused chaos and unleashed hatred, just as he had feared it would. Seven million Hindus and Sikhs had to take flight from the new Pakistani states, and a similar number of Muslims fled India amidst horrific scenes of mass riots, female abductions and rapes, and religiously motivated murders. Neighbor turned on neighbor and, instead of Gandhi's peaceful utopia, India became a bloodbath. Low estimates give the number of dead as 200,000.

The most famous victim of the partition was Gandhi himself. Nathuram Godse, a Hindu militant who abhorred Gandhi's advocacy of religious tolerance, shot him three times on his way into a prayer meeting on January 30, 1948. The Father of the Nation, who had led his country to independence through nonviolent means, was killed by a single act of supreme violence.

Gandhi's *satyagraha* influenced American pastor and social activist Martin Luther King, Jr., and he is still praised in almost saintly terms. His birthday is an Indian national holiday and the day of his death is observed as Martyrs' Day. ✠

# Martin Luther King, Jr.

## THE AMERICAN PASTOR WHO LED THE CAMPAIGN AGAINST RACIAL DISCRIMINATION BEFORE BEING ASSASSINATED

A white Mustang pulled up suddenly alongside the doorway to Canipe's Amusement Company and a man got out of the vehicle. He was white, 5ft 8in (1.7 m), slim, with cropped dark hair, and in his late thirties. He walked towards the building and dumped a large bundle outside. Then he jumped back into the Mustang and tore away. The bundle, the police discovered, contained binoculars, ammunition, and a .30-06 rifle. The man was James Earl Ray. He had just shot Martin Luther King, Jr., and would evade capture for two months.

**Opposite:** Reverend Martin Luther King, Jr. in 1964.

## FACT FILE

**Born:** January 15, 1929, Atlanta.
**Died:** April 4, 1968, Memphis.
**Historic Feat:** Led the civil rights movement to success in the US.
**Circumstances of Death:** Assassinated by white supremacist James Earl Ray.
**Legacy:** Often regarded as the greatest orator and civil rights campaigner in history.

King, born in Atlanta, Georgia on January 15, 1929, was perhaps the greatest orator in American history and used his speeches to garner support for the civil rights movement. In a climate of racial hatred and apartheid in some areas of the United States in the 1950s and 1960s, he mobilized mass demonstrations and edged the country toward legislation to ensure the equitable treatment of all citizens, black or white.

King was born to be a preacher and orator. He was a high-achieving student at Booker T. Washington High School, gained a degree in sociology, and went to seminary school in Pennsylvania to train for the Baptist ministry. In 1960, he became the third generation of his family

to become the pastor of the Ebenezer Baptist Church, Atlanta. By then he was already using his oratorical capabilities outside the walls of the church.

## RACIAL JUSTICE

The greatest social issue the young preacher tried to address was racial segregation, particularly in the Southern U.S. states. African Americans continued to be barred from most schools, libraries, hospitals, restaurants, bars, and cinemas, and suffered restrictive conditions on public transport. Meanwhile, institutionally racist police and judicial authorities repeatedly appeared to be complicit in covering up crimes and in failures to prosecute racist offenders.

By 1954, King was installed as the pastor of Dexter

Avenue Baptist Church in Montgomery, Alabama. At the end of the following year, on December 1, 1955, local resident Rosa Parks was arrested for refusing to give up her seat on a bus for a white man. King came to national prominence when he responded by leading an African American bus boycott in Montgomery. King personally endured a torrid time during the 385-day-long campaign. On January 30, 1956, his house was bombed while his wife Coretta and his daughter were home, but they were fortunately unharmed. King was arrested that year but his campaign ended in victory, with the U.S. Supreme Court banning segregation on Montgomery's public buses.

In 1957, King helped set up the Southern Christian Leadership Conference (SCLC) to tap into the collective campaigning power of churches across the Southern states. King was appointed the SCLC president, a post he held until his death just over a decade later. During that time, he became one of the most notable political figures in the United States through his nonviolent campaign against discrimination. He made more than 2,500 speeches and traveled around the globe on behalf of the cause. The animosity of some whites, especially in the Southern states, grew in parallel to his fame. As well as being assaulted, he was arrested more than twenty times.

On October 22, 1960, he was sentenced to four months hard labor on the charge of driving with the wrong state license. It seemed clear that some members of the authorities were out to suppress his voice. Despite never publicly endorsing either of the main parties, King had a powerful ally. The young Democrat John F. Kennedy, who would be inaugurated as president in January 1961, arranged King's release through his brother Bobby Kennedy.

## "I HAVE A DREAM"

The summit of King's career was yet to come. In the Great March on Washington, D.C., on August 28, 1963, 200,000 people walked from the Washington Monument to the Lincoln Memorial in the name of the civil rights movement. The event concluded with what remains one of the most famous speeches in history: "I have a dream," King said to the enraptured crowd. "I have a dream that one day my four little children will live in a nation where they will not be judged by the color of their skin but by the content of their character."

The mass march helped beget a new era for the civil rights movement. Stokely Carmichael's Student Nonviolent Coordinating Committee mobilized almost constant student action, involving sit-ins and protests across the south. President Kennedy was now willing to face the ire of many white Southern Democrats and started the process of creating civil rights legislation, outlawing racial discrimination and segregation. Kennedy was assassinated in November 1963, but his successor President Lyndon B. Johnson pushed ahead and the Civil Rights Act became law in July 1964.

By then, King's nonviolent campaigning had made him an international hero. In October 1964, he became the youngest person in history to receive the Nobel Peace Prize. He was only 35. He then widened his platform to campaign against poverty and the Vietnam War.

**Above:** King waves to some of the 250,000 participants of the March on Washington from the Lincoln Memorial, where he delivered his "I Have a Dream" speech on August 28, 1963.
**Opposite:** President John F. Kennedy.

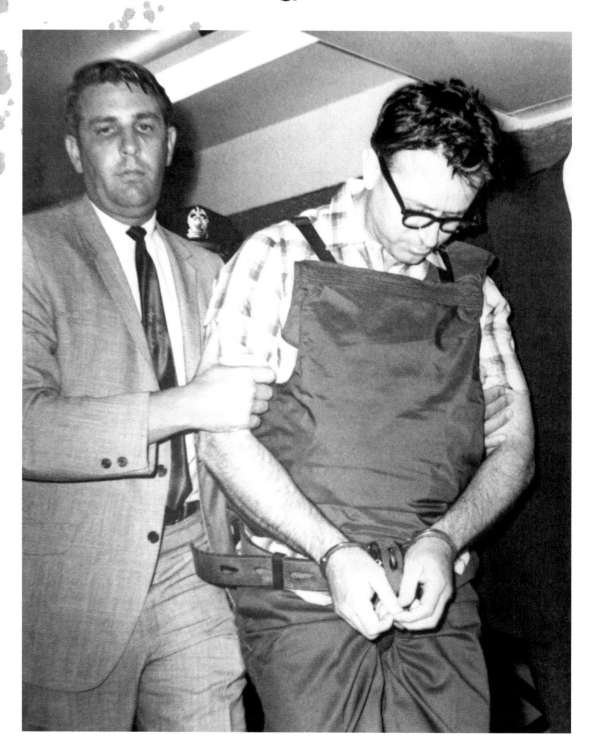

## MALCOLM X

Despite the acclaim, King was never free of enemies. On April 4, 1968, King was standing on the balcony of a hotel in Memphis. A single bullet suddenly smashed his jaw, hit his spinal cord and shuddered into his shoulder, killing one of the greatest figures in American history.

The white supremacist and convicted armed robber James Earl Ray escaped the scene and was on the run for two months before being arrested at Heathrow Airport, London. He pleaded guilty to the assassination but the retraction of his confession, and a lack of substantial evidence, have fueled conspiracy theories ever since. King's short but immensely significant life is celebrated with a U.S. public holiday in January each year. ✤

**Opposite:** James Earl Ray, the assassin of Martin Luther King, Jr.
**Above (left):** NBC News image of the March on Washington.
**Above (right):** King and Malcolm X in 1964, the only time they met.

WHEN it came to civil rights action, Malcolm X provided an alternative approach to the nonviolence of Martin Luther King, Jr. Instead of supporting desegregation, the former convict and member of African American group Nation of Islam (born Malcolm Little on May 19, 1925) was a black supremacist and separatist who wanted to be free of the white race of "devils." An impressive orator, he called the March on Washington, D.C., the "farce on Washington," advocated violent resistance to white domination, and wanted to create a black nation within America. By 1964, his opinions had become less radical and had turned against the Nation of Islam. He was assassinated in Harlem, New York, by members of the Nation of Islam on February 21, 1965.

# Bernie Madoff

## THE FINANCIAL SCAMMER RESPONSIBLE FOR WHAT IS CONSIDERED THE BIGGEST PONZI SCHEME (INVESTMENT FRAUD) IN US HISTORY

**B**ernard L. Madoff was a great philanthropist and he was a miracle worker when it came to investment returns. He was trustworthy, too; after all, he had been the nonexecutive chairman of the NASDAQ stock exchange. Yet Bernie was also a crook. For years, he operated one of the largest scams in financial history. He risked the wealth of others, including charities, on a fragile house of cards that inevitably came tumbling down. In the aftermath, financial institutions, courts, and media were left to sieve through the mess to work out just how Madoff's Ponzi scheme had gone undetected. (A Ponzi scheme is an investment scam in which those who invest early are paid off by later investors, with the intention of encouraging bigger and bigger investments.)

**Opposite:** Bernard Madoff leaves the federal courthouse in New York. He pled guilty to securities fraud, perjury, and making false filings to the SEC on March 12, 2009.

## CREDENTIALS

Madoff was not a shifty operator dragging the gullible into a dubious get-rich-quick scheme. He was positioned close to the heart of the financial establishment. His company, Bernard L. Madoff Investment Securities LLC, which included various Madoff family members on its staff, had been operating since 1960. It had been built up over the course of nearly fifty years to be counted amongst the very best market-maker companies on Wall Street. However, for around twenty years the firm also operated a fraudulent investment management service that offered exceptional rates of return based on a web of lies.

As far as investors in the investment service were concerned, Madoff ran an esteemed company with an excellent, proven record. As well as Bernard serving as NASDAQ's chairman, the family was heavily involved in the Security Industries and Financial Markets

### FACT FILE

**Born:** April 29, 1938, Queens, New York.

**Historic Feat:** Ran the biggest financial scam in U.S. history.

**Legacy:** Charities and foundations were severely damaged by lost investments; financial regulation authorities were weakened by the scandal.

Association (SIFMA): his brother Peter was on the board and his niece Shana was on its compliance & legal division committee. Madoff's website boasted what appeared to be a guarantee of propriety: "Clients know that Bernard Madoff has a personal interest in maintaining an unblemished record of value, fair-dealing, and high ethical standards that has always been the firm's hallmark."

That claim was supported by Madoff's reputation as a leading philanthropist. He had donated $6 million to lymphoma research after his son Andrew was diagnosed

**Above:** Harry Markopolos, who repeatedly asked the SEC to investigate Madoff.
**Opposite:** Wall Street, the hub of American finance, was damaged by the biggest Ponzi scandal in history.

with the condition, and made significant donations to charities, hospitals, and cultural institutions through his foundation. When Madoff offered returns significantly above the industry norm, charities and foundations had no reason to suspect that this was down to anything but Madoff's financial ingenuity and long-standing experience.

What they did not know was that a financial analyst named Harry Markopolos had been repeatedly asking the U.S. Securities and Exchange Commission (SEC) to investigate Madoff since 2000. He knew that the returns Madoff claimed to be able to deliver to his investors just did not add up. However, the SEC dropped the matter, with Madoff later saying, "They never even looked at my stock records." Markopolos was not alone in his suspicions. None of the major Wall Street and derivatives firms traded with Madoff's investment division: they knew that his figures were mathematically untenable.

## COLLAPSE

In 2008, it all came tumbling down. Madoff confided that he was having difficulty raising $7 billion in redemptions to investors, yet simultaneously wanted to pay out $173 million in bonuses to staff—primarily family members—two months early. Madoff knew that the end was near and the company was about to collapse. His sons Mark and Andrew confronted him on December 10, 2008, and Madoff confessed that his entire investment operation was just "one big lie," and there were no funds left because it was "one giant Ponzi scheme." The brothers apparently immediately reported Bernie to the authorities and on December 11 Madoff was arrested for fraud.

Madoff later admitted to the authorities that the investment scheme was a scam. Rather than investing his clients' money and generating returns, he would simply pay it into an account at Chase Manhattan bank; when clients

were due a return or wanted their money, "I used the money in the Chase Manhattan bank account that belonged to them or other clients to pay the requested funds." Meanwhile, his staff apparently concocted false trading reports to show clients, matching the level of return that had been promised to them. Meanwhile, Madoff took his cut of the supposed trading success. The scheme collapsed when the level of redemptions at a given time exceeded the funds in the Chase account.

## CONSEQUENCES

The scam came at a huge cost to some of the investors: $17.3 billion in real money invested by clients was owed, along with another $40 million in fictitious returns. Some funds have been recovered, but there is likely to remain a shortfall of $10 to $15 billion in real money. The victims included the Lappin Charitable Foundation for Jewish youth, which was temporarily forced to close because almost its entire endowment ($8 billion) had been invested with Madoff. Movie director Steven Spielberg's charitable Wunderkinder Foundation was among many charities, federations, and hospitals to be severely damaged.

Madoff was sentenced to 150 years in prison, and the SEC and other institutions faced damning questions about their inability to detect a Ponzi scheme that had been running since at least 1991. However, it was Madoff's son Mark who perhaps paid the biggest price for the largest financial fraud in American history: he hanged himself on the second anniversary of his father's arrest. ✛

# MURDER
## &
# MAYHEM

# Blackbeard

## THE INFAMOUS EIGHTEENTH-CENTURY PIRATE WHO SCOURED THE CARIBBEAN AND THE AMERICAN EAST COAST FOR VICTIMS AND LOOT

The merchant ship was assaulted by a broadside of cannon before the pirate vessel drew alongside with grapple hooks—and its fighting men poured on board. In the chaos of musket fire, grenades, smoke, and slashing blades, one man could be made out, standing unusually tall, with cutlass in one hand and pistol in the other. It was Blackbeard, the pirate feared more than any other by the merchant seamen. Most of his face was covered by a long, black beard, its sections twisted with ribbons so they stuck out. Lit cords soaked in saltpeter hung down from his hat, yet the smoke did not obscure his wild expression. He uttered his booming war cry as he strode toward the helmsman, but the sailor chose the sea over certain death and jumped

**Opposite:** Blackbeard, depicted shortly after his death in *A General History of the Robberies and Murders of the Most Notorious Pirates* by Captain Charles Johnson (aka Daniel Defoe).

## FACT FILE

**Born:** c. 1680, Bristol.
**Died:** November 22, 1718, Ocracoke.
**Historic Feat:** Plundered merchant ships in the Caribbean and off the East Coast of America.
**Circumstances of Death:** Killed by a pirate hunter.
**Legacy:** The most infamous pirate in history who partly inspired *The Pirates of the Caribbean.*

overboard. Yet another ship, and all its cargo, had fallen into Blackbeard's hands. He had terrorized the Caribbean and East Coast of America for two years, and it seemed that no one could stop him.

Blackbeard was the stuff of legend even while he was still alive and his reputation was so fierce that many merchant sea captains gave up their precious booty without a fight.

His real name is believed to have been Edward Teach and he was born around 1680 in Bristol, England, but he would make his huge fortune thousands of miles away.

## IN QUEEN ANNE'S SERVICE

To begin with, his scandalous actions were condoned because he was a privateer acting in the interests of Queen Anne of England. The War of the Spanish Succession raged between England, France, and Spain from 1701, and the fighting quickly

spread to the countries' holdings in the Caribbean. Private sea captains and sailors such as Teach were not an official part of the English navy, but their attacks on ships in the West Indies and the theft of their cargo helped weaken the resources of England's enemies. Once the war concluded in 1714, the privateers no longer had an official role to play, but the captains and crews pursued the same lucrative policy of capturing ships and looting their holds. The privateers were now pirates, and no ships were safe.

From around 1716, Teach served under the pirate Benjamin Thornigold who plagued merchant ships around New Providence in the Bahamas. With Blackbeard commanding one of his sloops, Thornigold stole cargo including flour, wine, spirits, and, rarely, gold bullion. After 1717, Thornigold switched sides and

**Above:** Blackbeard was allegedly wounded twenty-five times in the battle with Lieutenant Robert Maynard's men; the final blow decapitated him.
**Opposite:** Blackbeard's decapitated head hanging off the bowsprit of Maynard's ship.

became a pirate hunter, but Teach's career was yet to reach its zenith. Teach captured a large French merchant ship and converted it into a formidable, 40-gun warship he named *Queen Anne's Revenge*.

## THE LEGEND OF BLACKBEARD

A domineering, ruthless man, Edward Teach was now a pirate captain and the legend of Blackbeard, the most frightening pirate ever to sail the seas, was born. He soon garnered a reputation for cruelty: merchant seamen would be cut to ribbons when Blackbeard boarded their ships, and there were reports of disembowelments as well as passengers having their fingers cut off to free their rings. One captive was reputedly forced to eat his own amputated ears. According to Charles Ellms, writing in 1837, Blackbeard married a 16-year-old girl, "his fourteenth wife, about twelve of whom were yet alive; and though this woman was young and amiable, he behaved toward her in a manner so brutal, that it was shocking to all decency and propriety."

Blackbeard spent the winter hounding ships in the

Caribbean, but in the summer based the *Queen Anne's Revenge* and his other captured vessels in the Ocracoke Inlet on the North Carolina coast. There he would pick off the easy prey of merchant vessels trading with the ports of Virginia and Carolina. In May 1718, he blockaded the harbor of Charleston, South Carolina, crippling trade in the region. Nine vessels were looted and a group of wealthy citizens on their way to London were taken prisoner. Blackbeard threatened to behead them and to burn all the captured ships unless he received medical supplies from Charleston. His demand was met and he released the prisoners, but not before he had humiliated them by stripping them of their fine clothes and jewelry.

## THE PIRATE HUNTED

By then English patience with the rogue pirate had worn thin. The English supported Alexander Spotswood, the governor of Virginia, in his attempts to capture Blackbeard, dead or alive. In November 1718, two ships commanded by Lieutenant Robert Maynard were sent straight towards Ocracoke to flush out Blackbeard's men.

The pirate was a capable captain and caught Maynard's

vessels in a thundering broadside. In response, Maynard employed a touch of piratical sleight of hand by luring Blackbeard onto the decks of his main ship in the belief that most of the men had been killed. Maynard then sprang an ambush from the hold. Charles Johnson (aka Daniel Defoe), writing shortly afterwards, claimed the surrounded pirate "stood his ground and fought with great fury till he received five and twenty wounds." The last blow separated his head from his shoulders.

Blackbeard's severed head was dangled from the bowsprit of Maynard's ship to warn other pirates of their fate. Nonetheless, the Golden Age of Piracy continued off the American East Coast and in the Caribbean for another decade, not least because more criminals wanted to emulate the infamous Blackbeard and reap similar rewards.

## FEMALE PIRATES

**PIRACY in the seventeenth and eighteenth centuries was not the preserve of males: both Mary Read and Anne Bonny were fonder of a cutlass than a corset and became two of the most notorious pirates of the Golden Age of Piracy. Englishwoman Mary Read, better known as "Mark," dressed as a boy from childhood and fought as a male soldier in Europe. In 1720, she joined the same pirate crew as Irishwoman Anne Bonny in the Caribbean. Once, when their ship was boarded by pirate hunters, only the women stayed on deck to fight while the male pirates cowered in the hold. Read was arrested and died in prison in 1721.**

# Dick Turpin

## THE MOST FAMOUS EIGHTEENTH-CENTURY HIGHWAYMAN, WHO HARRIED WEALTHY TRAVELERS TO GIVE UP THEIR JEWELS

The atmosphere inside the stagecoach was already tense. Anyone traveling the highways around London knew they were under threat from the mysterious highwayman who was plaguing the roads. The four travelers—including a governess and her young ward—were sitting opposite each other, cramped and sweating. They looked at each other with startled expressions as they heard hoofs rapidly gaining on the carriage. They all lurched as the coach suddenly stopped and the horses reared. "Down," they heard a male voice order the coachman. They knew they were doomed. Their valuables would be stripped from them. The best they could hope for from the oncoming ordeal

**Opposite:** The highwayman Dick Turpin is often depicted as a handsome, gallant rogue rather than as a callous murderer with a pockmarked face.

## ✎ FACT FILE ✎

**Born:** September 25, 1705, Essex.
**Died:** April 7, 1739, York.
**Historic Feat:** Highwayman, thief, and murderer who became famous in eighteenth-century England.
**Circumstances of Death:** Hanged having been found guilty of horse stealing.
**Legacy:** Romanticized as a courageous, dashing highwayman, Turpin became a legendary figure of English folklore.

was to emerge with their lives—and chastity—intact. Their fates now lay in the hands of Dick Turpin, the most famous and feared highway robber in the history of England.

Turpin was not just feared: he was a romantic figure whose history would be twisted into legends, not least that he rode his faithful mount from London to York, a distance of 200 miles (320 km), in twenty-four hours. In reality, that feat was the work of another highwayman, John Nevison, who made the journey in 1676 to establish a false alibi. Turpin may be associated with tales of derring-do and charming nonchalance in the face of death, but he mostly led the sordid life of a common thief.

Richard "Dick" Turpin was born in Essex in 1705, but as a teenager moved toward the edge of London to become a butcher's apprentice in

Whitechapel. Never a young man of high virtue, when he set up his own shop he saved himself a fortune by stealing animals to slaughter and sell. The romantic view of Turpin was that he was a lone highwayman, willing to single-handedly defy the law. In fact, Turpin was originally part of a criminal posse, the Essex Gang.

To begin with, their modus operandi was to poach deer and attack houses, rather than coaches. They extorted valuables through violent threats and torture, and Turpin was often their lead interrogator. He once held a brave old woman over a fire until her son squealed and gave up her entire fortune—an image at odds with that of a debonair, swashbuckling rogue so charming that some young women were meant actively to want to be ravaged by him.

The Essex Gang's reputation for cruelty grew and a bounty of £50 was put on their heads in 1735. Members of the notorious gang were soon captured and hanged, and Turpin went into hiding.

## LIFE AS A HIGHWAY ROBBER

Turpin was soon working as a highwayman, sometimes linking up with an accomplice called Matthew King. They would watch a stretch of Essex road in Epping Forest and swoop on isolated travelers. The image of him with carbine raised and sultry, appreciative eyes as he freed wealthy female travelers of their jewels belies the fact that many of his victims were peddlers with carts.

Turpin then made a series of mistakes. In 1737, he forced

a traveler to give him his horse on the road to London; but he had picked the wrong man. The victim circulated handbills with a detailed description of the stolen steed. Turpin stabled the horse at an inn in his old stomping ground of Whitechapel, ready for King to collect. King was set upon by waiting constables and, allegedly, Turpin fired at them. The highwayman was not so good a shot as legend suggests: he supposedly killed King.

Turpin's victims were so numerous that the reward on his head eventually grew to £100. It was enough money to encourage bounty hunters and one, an armed gamekeeper called Thomas Morris, apprehended Turpin in the forest. The highwayman simply raised his carbine and shot him. The thief, vagabond, and highwayman was now a horse thief and murderer. If he was caught for either offense, he would hang.

Turpin hid out in Epping Forest, but he knew he would never be safe in the area. He moved to Brough in Yorkshire, giving rise to the confusion about the twenty-four-hour horse ride to York. Under the assumed name of John Palmer, he recommenced his criminal activities of stealing horses and committing highway robbery.

His carelessness and violent temper soon gave the game away. He shot a man's rooster in the street and then threatened the life of the man himself. He was arrested and eventually thrown in the dungeon at York, and the authorities began to realize that "John Palmer" was associated with a roster of other crimes. His true identity was unearthed by bizarre coincidence. He sent a letter to his brother-in-law in Essex, who refused to pay the postage due, so the letter was returned to the Post Office. There, Turpin's former teacher recognized the writing as that of the highwayman. The magistrate dispatched the man to identify the sender, "John Palmer," as none other than Dick Turpin.

At his execution by hanging at York racecourse on April 7, 1739, Turpin finally acted in the courageous manner

THE
# TRIAL
Of the Notorious Highwayman
## Richard Turpin,

At *York* Assizes, on the 22d Day of *March*, 1739, before the Hon. Sir WILLIAM CHAPPLE, Kt. Judge of Assize, and one of His Majesty's Justices of the Court of King's Bench.

Taken down in Court by Mr. THOMAS KYLL, Professor of Short Hand.

To which is prefix'd,

An exact Account of the said *Turpin*, from his first coming into *Yorkshire*, to the Time of his being committed Prisoner to *York* Castle; communicated by Mr. APPLETON of *Beverley*, Clerk of the Peace for the *East-Riding* of the said County.

With a Copy of a Letter which *Turpin* received from his Father, while under Sentence of Death.

To which is added,

His Behaviour at the Place of Execution, on *Saturday* the 7th of *April*, 1739. Together with the whole Confession he made to the Hangman at the Gallows; wherein he acknowledg'd himself guilty of the Facts for which he suffer'd, own'd the Murder of Mr. *Thompson's* Servant on *Epping-Forest*, and gave a particular Account of several Robberies which he had committed.

legend has accorded him. He had bought new clothes for the occasion and, according to the *Gentleman's Magazine*, "behaved in an undaunted manner; as he mounted the ladder, feeling his right leg tremble, he spoke a few words to the topsman, then threw himself off." The legend of "Dauntless Dick Turpin," the most famous highwayman in history, was born, and the thief, torturer, and murderer would become the hero of countless romantic ballads and stories. ❧

**Opposite:** Turpin repeatedly evaded capture until he was imprisoned in Yorkshire in 1738.

**Above:** The title page of a pamphlet published in York following the execution of Dick Turpin, 1739.

# Thug Behram

## THE EIGHTEENTH- TO NINETEENTH-CENTURY INDIAN KILLER ALLEGED TO HAVE STRANGLED NEARLY 1,000 PEOPLE

The old man forced his victim feet first into the deep hole and buried him until only his head and neck were above the surface. With a fervent gleam in his eye, Thug Behram then circled his ceremonial cloth around the traveler's neck and began to cut off his air supply, ignoring his desperate choking noises until the strangulation was complete. Behram had fulfilled his holy duty, but he completed the act by carefully putting the ceremonial cloth over his victim's motionless face. He was the 931st victim of the 75-year-old killer, but he would be his last.

Behram (or Buhram) Jemedar's career as the most prolific serial killer in history began fifty years earlier in 1790 when he was around 25 years

old and joined the notorious Thuggee cult. A drawing of Behram reveals him to be a handsome, mustachioed man, and the portrait offers no hint of the carnage he was willing to inflict. Little is known of Behram's early life, but he may have been a Shia Muslim of Persian descent, whose family settled in Awadh, northern India. He later married a Sunni Muslim. After joining the Thuggee gang, Behram showed the necessary murderous aptitude to become their leader. Rather than merely executing and burying the victims, it seems that he would sometimes bury his living victims up to their neck before murdering them by asphyxiation.

First records of the existence of the Thuggee cult date back to 1356. Although they originated among Muslim tribes, the Thuggees became associated with Hinduism. Their name derived from the Hindu word for "thief" and they roamed

**Opposite:** The Thuggees took thousands of lives in honor of the Hindu goddess Kali.

## FACT FILE

**Born:** c. 1765, Awadh.
**Died:** 1840, Jabalpur.
**Historic Feat:** Linked to murders of 931 people.
**Circumstances of Death:** Hanged by the British administration in India.
**Legacy:** Probably the most prolific serial killer in history; the Thuggee cult of assassins was wiped out by 1870.

the countryside looking for isolated caravans of travelers; the victims would be dispatched through strangulation using either a *rumal* (a large head-covering or kerchief) or a noose before their valuables were taken and their bodies buried or thrown down a well.

In the 1830s, with India under British control, the country's Governor-General Lord Cavendish-Bentinck and his administrator Sir William Sleeman made it their ambition to destroy the secret Thuggee sect. Figures vary wildly, but the historian Mike Dash estimates that the Thuggees had been responsible for more than 50,000 murders in the previous 150 years. Sleeman managed to capture a leading Thuggee known as "Feringhea," who had led him to the grave of 100 travelers, before he turned his attention to Behram Jemedar, "King of the Thugs."

## IN HONOR OF KALI

The Thuggees excused their murderous actions as a religious undertaking. Behram and his personal band of Thuggees, which numbered up to fifty men with half-a-dozen designated murderers, believed that they were saving humanity by taking lives on behalf of Kali, the Hindu goddess associated with destruction.

The Thuggees claimed they were the children of Kali, made from her sweat. Behram used a *rumal*, which he reputedly wore as a cummerbund around his waist, as his tool of execution. The cloth had a large metal medallion sewn into it and, during an execution, Thug Behram would carefully position the medallion over his victim's Adam's apple so that it would cut off their air supply. The medallion, no doubt plundered from a particularly wealthy traveler, featured the Italian sculptor Antonio Canova (1757–1822) on one side and his most famous work, *The Three Graces*, on the other.

Sleeman, who had more than 1,400 Thuggees executed or exiled to penal colonies during his campaign, finally caught Behram and imprisoned him at Jabalpur in 1840. In order to make Behram confess, Sleeman arranged to bring his son Ali from Awadh, and, fearing that his son would be executed alongside him, Behram confessed to his crimes and informed on his fellow Thuggees. According to James Paton, an officer of the East India Company (which formed the British administration) who gave an account of Behram's confession in *Collections on Thuggee and Dacoitee*, Behram admitted to being present at an incredible 931 murders. However, somewhat confusingly, Behram is also quoted as saying, "I may have strangled with my own hands about 125 men and may have seen strangled 150 more." Whatever Behram's individual involvement in each of the murders, even the lowest figure marks him out as one of the most prolific serial killers in history.

Sleeman wanted to reclaim the Thuggees' supposed hoards of stolen goods. It has been alleged that although Ali helped officers from the East India Company unearth several caches, much of the stolen treasure was privately pocketed by officials.

Behram's final act was to clear his own son from any blame: "My son Ali whom you have detained was never initiated into the Thuggee fold. I request the honorable magistrate to please let him return to his mother in Awadh." Despite informing on his colleagues, Behram was sentenced to death and hanged. The Canova medallion that was attached to the *rumal* was passed down through his descendants and is now held in a private collection in Bangalore.

By 1870, largely due to the actions of Sleeman, the Thuggee cult had been destroyed. Meanwhile, the word "thug," used to describe a violent or aggressive person, had already passed into the English language.

**Above:** Multhoo Byragee Jogee, a 90-year-old convicted Thuggee, drawn by Colesworthy Grant in the mid-nineteenth century.
**Opposite:** Watercolor by an unknown artist from the early nineteenth century showing three Thuggees strangling a traveler.

# John Wilkes Booth

## THE PRO-SLAVERY ASSASSIN OF ABRAHAM LINCOLN, PRESIDENT OF THE UNITED STATES

John Wilkes Booth was an acclaimed actor, but as he stood nervously awaiting his big moment during the performance of *Our American Cousin* at Ford's Theatre, Washington, D.C., it was not because he was about to take the stage. The spotlight was going to turn on him for a final time solely because he held in his palm a .44 caliber Philadelphia Deringer handgun. At 10:15 p.m. on April 14, 1865, Booth was going to enter a theater box and assassinate the president of the United States.

John Wilkes Booth, born on May 10, 1838, in Bel Air, Maryland, was the son of an English Shakespearean actor, Junius Brutus Booth, and

**Opposite:** The assassination of Abraham Lincoln as he watched a performance at Ford's Theatre, Washington, D.C., on April 14, 1865.

## FACT FILE

**Born:** May 10, 1838, Bel Air, Maryland.

**Died:** April 26, 1865, Port Royal, Virginia.

**Historic Feat:** Assassinated Abraham Lincoln, 16th president of the United States of America.

**Circumstances of Death:** Booth was tracked down in an army manhunt and shot. His co-conspirators David Herold, Lewis Powell, and George Atzerodt were hanged.

**Legacy:** The assassination of Lincoln did nothing for the Confederate cause and Lincoln remains a national hero.

named after a liberal English politician—none of which suggested that Booth would become an out-and-out Confederate or a presidential assassin. However, when he was a boy, John Wilkes had his palm read by a fortune-teller who informed him that she had "never seen a worst hand:" he was destined to lead a grand but short life, be beset with trouble, and "make a bad end." In the event, he would become one of the most famous assassins in history.

## STRONG SUPPORTER OF SLAVERY

Booth followed his father into the acting profession and found success in Richmond, Virginia, where he adopted typically Southern views on slavery. In 1859, he was amongst the armed militiamen who ensured that no one could rescue John Brown, the abolitionist who had attempted

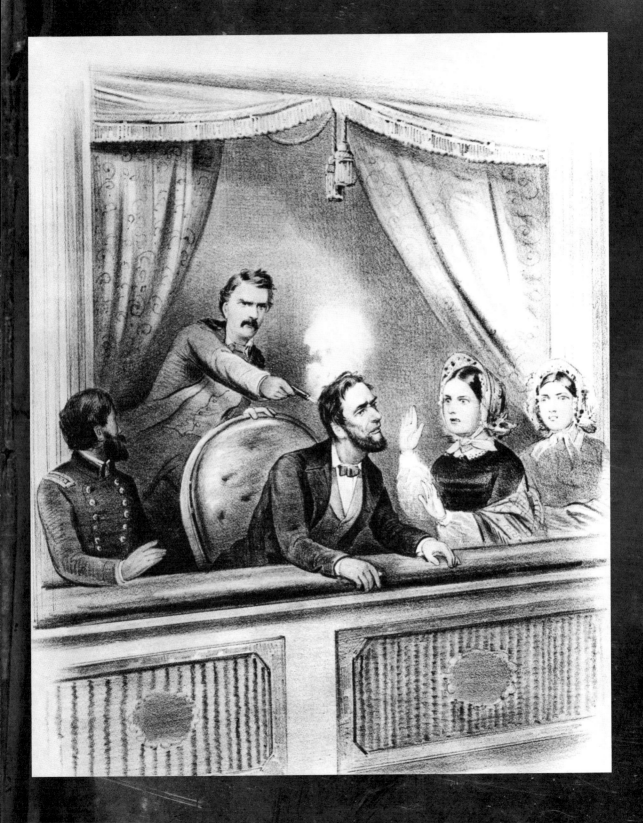

to mount an armed slave uprising, from hanging. Booth was increasingly disgusted by the rise of the abolitionist movement and developed a deep hatred for its leading man, President Abraham Lincoln. He would later write to his brother-in-law, "This country was formed for the white not for the black man," and believed slavery to be "one of the greatest blessings (both for themselves and us) God ever bestowed upon a favored nation."

Booth supported the Confederate states from the beginning of the American Civil War in 1861, and in 1863 was fined for making anti-government remarks. Later that year, Lincoln saw Booth perform in *The Marble Heart* at

## U.S. PRESIDENTIAL ASSASSINATIONS

Abraham Lincoln, 16th president, shot by John Wilkes Booth on April 14, 1865; died April 15, 1865.

James A. Garfield, 20th president, shot by Charles J. Giteau on July 2, 1881; died September 19, 1881.

William McKinley, 25th president, shot by Leon Czolgosz on September 6, 1901; died September 14, 1901.

John F. Kennedy, 35th president, shot by Lee Harvey Oswald on November 22, 1963; died November 22, 1963.

Two other presidents are rumored to have been poisoned:

Zachary Taylor, 12th president, died on July 9, 1850.

Warren G. Harding, 29th president, died on August 2, 1923. The main suspect for Harding's poisoning was his own wife.

Ford's Theatre in Washington and noticed that the actor, who was playing a villain, delivered his most threatening lines directly to him. Booth kept a promise to his mother not to fight during the war, and instead started scheming to have a greater impact on the future of the United States than any single Confederate soldier could effect. He would kidnap the president.

He gathered together a band of conspirators including David Herold, Lewis Powell, and George Atzerodt. Knowing that Lincoln was due to attend a theater performance just outside Washington in March 1865, they hatched a plot to intercept the president's carriage and take him hostage; he would then be exchanged for huge numbers of Confederate prisoners held in Union jails. The plot fell apart when Lincoln changed his plans. In fact, the entire Confederate cause was about to receive a fatal blow with the surrender of General Lee on April 9.

Nonetheless, Booth's unswerving devotion to the anti-abolitionist cause did not falter and he was incensed when Lincoln declared that some blacks should be given voting rights. A few days later, on April 14, Booth was at Ford's Theatre, picking up his mail, when he learned that Lincoln would be attending a showing of *Our American Cousin* there that evening. Booth knew exactly where Lincoln would be sitting. He no longer wanted to kidnap the president. He wanted to kill him.

## CONSPIRACY AGAINST THE PRESIDENT

Booth quickly sought out his fellow-conspirators and hatched a plan to devastate the abolitionists' legislative plans. At 10:15 that evening—the time Booth planned to assassinate the president—George Atzerodt would simultaneously kill Vice President Andrew Johnson and Lewis Powell would assassinate Secretary of State William Seward elsewhere in Washington.

Booth fulfilled his side of the deal. Just after 10:15, he stepped through the rear door of the theater box, placed the muzzle of his gun behind Lincoln's left ear and pulled the trigger. As Lincoln slumped forward, someone tried to wrestle Booth to the ground, but Booth stabbed his assailant and jumped over the box's rail and onto the stage, seemingly breaking his ankle in the process. Some audience members later claimed that they heard him shout in Latin, "*Sic temper tyrannis*" ("Thus always to tyrants"), the words Brutus allegedly used when he assassinated the dictator Julius Caesar in 44 BC. Despite his injury, Booth managed to exit the back of the theater and ride away on horseback. He was joined by co-conspirator David Herold and they spent the next twelve days on the run. Meanwhile, Powell stabbed Seward, who survived, but Atzerodt lost his nerve and never attempted to kill the vice president.

The Union cavalry tracked Booth and Herold down to a tobacco farm in Virginia on 26 April. Herold surrendered but Booth held out, so the soldiers torched the barn to flush him out and shot him. While dying, Booth looked at his hands and said, "Useless! Useless!"

Perhaps not. After all, he achieved his first aim: Lincoln had died on the morning after Booth shot him. The greater aim, though, did end in failure. On December 18, 1865, Seward proclaimed the adoption of the Thirteenth Amendment to the U.S. Constitution, abolishing slavery and involuntary servitude throughout the United States. ⏁

**Above:** President Abraham Lincoln (left) and his assassin, the actor John Wilkes Booth (right).

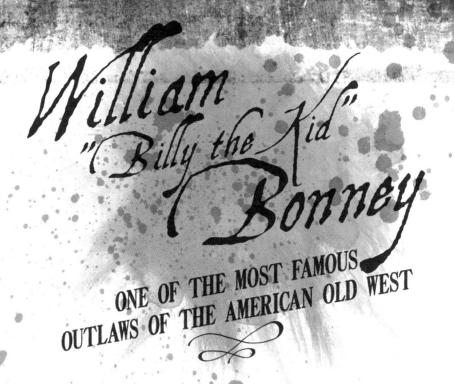

# William "Billy the Kid" Bonney

## ONE OF THE MOST FAMOUS OUTLAWS OF THE AMERICAN OLD WEST

William Henry McCarty, Jr. would become better known as the legendary William H. Bonney or Billy the Kid, the outlaw, villain, and folk hero. Little is known about his early years, but the blond, blue-eyed boy was born to an Irish-American mother in New York City in 1859 and lived in the poverty-stricken slums of the city. Fatherless, he headed west with his mother Catherine to seek better fortune, and reached Silver City in New Mexico in 1873. By then, his mother had married the much younger William Antrim, but Billy rarely used his stepfather's surname. A year later, Catherine was dead from

**Opposite:** The only authenticated photograph of the notorious outlaw William Henry McCarty, Jr., better known as William H. Bonney or Billy the Kid, c. 1879.

### ☙ FACT FILE ❧

**Born:** November 23, 1859, New York.

**Died:** July 14, 1881, Fort Sumner.

**Historic Feat:** Outlaw who killed between eight and twenty-one people in the Old West.

**Circumstances of Death:** Tracked down by Sheriff Pat Garrett after escaping a courthouse while facing execution.

**Legacy:** The most famous young outlaw of the Old West.

illness, and the boy had been arrested several times for theft.

Billy, a slight teenager, worked as a ranch-hand in Arizona, but stepped up his criminal activities to include horse theft. According to folklore, he supposedly killed the first of up to twenty-one victims when he was still only 17 years old, during an altercation with a bullying blacksmith in Fort Grant in August 1877. Later that year, he turned up in Lincoln County, New Mexico, bearing the pseudonym William H. Bonney, which might suggest that young Billy really did have something to hide. If so, he failed to be discreet. The remaining four years of his life were filled with murder and mayhem.

Lincoln County was not the best place to be for a law-abiding citizen, but it was heaven for those that loved lawlessness and gunfights. An English

## BUTCH CASSIDY

ONE man who could rival Billy the Kid as the most famous outlaw of the Old West was Butch Cassidy (1866–1908). A Mormon born Robert Parker in 1866, he was soon following a life of crime. He was part of the notorious Wild Bunch Gang, who were responsible for bank and train robberies, as well as the deaths of multiple lawmen. The gang used to hide out in the famous Hole-in-the-Wall in Wyoming. With Pinkerton detectives on their tail, Cassidy and Harry "the Sundance Kid" Longabaugh fled to Bolivia. In 1908, following a payroll robbery, they were surrounded in a house by soldiers and badly shot up; one of them (no one knows which) shot the other to put him out of his misery and then committed suicide.

rancher and trader, John Tunstall, had armed himself with a team of gun-wielding cattlemen and ranch-hands, called the Regulators, to get the upper hand against rivals in what became known as the Lincoln County War. Billy the Kid became one of those ranch hands and grew close to Tunstall, perhaps seeing in him a father figure. Whatever the relationship, when the local sheriff and his posse, all supposedly in the pay of Tunstall's rivals, killed the rancher in an ambush, Billy was intent on exacting a very bloody revenge.

Top of the list were the rogue sheriff and his deputy. Billy was not a subtle young man: he and the Regulators fixed an ambush and mowed them down on Lincoln's main street. Billy was now an outlaw. More gunfights and murders occurred around Lincoln as U.S. cavalrymen became involved in the bitter conflict. Billy the Kid, already a famed marksman, fled initially to Texas and then ran the authorities ragged for two years, repeatedly evading capture; he allegedly killed a man in a saloon in Fort Sumner, New Mexico. By 1880, the governor of New Mexico had placed a $500 bounty on Bonney's head, but it would take more than an ordinary man to capture the young villain.

Pat Garrett was no ordinary man. If Billy the Kid was set to become one of the Old West's most legendary outlaws, Patrick Floyd Garrett would be its most famous sheriff. A smalltime rancher and former buffalo hunter, Garrett already knew Billy from his time working as a bartender, and he was just as quick on the draw. He was elected sheriff of Lincoln County in November

**Opposite:** Billy the Kid shooting a bartender in 1880, illustrated in the *Police Gazette*.

1880 with the remit to return the county to a state of lawfulness. There was only one place to start: the capture of William Bonney. In December, he raised a posse and caught Billy near Fort Sumner, almost 150 miles (240 km) from Lincoln, and the young outlaw was convicted for the murder of the former sheriff.

## DARING ESCAPE

Billy was held at Lincoln's courthouse awaiting execution by hanging. On April 28, 1881, when Garrett was out of town, Billy managed to break free while returning from using the

**Above (left):** The gravestone of Billy the Kid in Fort Sumner, New Mexico, where he was tracked down and killed in 1881.
**Above (right):** Portrait of Pat F. Garrett, the sheriff who shot Billy the Kid.
**Opposite:** The jail and courthouse in Lincoln, New Mexico, where Billy the Kid was held.

bathroom: he grabbed a revolver and shot his guard; another guard ran from across the street in the direction of the gunfire, but he too was mown down by the Kid. Billy then fled full gallop out of town.

Garrett, it seems, was a patient man. Billy may have been handy with a six-shooter, but he was not good at keeping quiet. Sooner or later, Garrett would hear of his whereabouts, and in the meantime he calmly tended to his ranch. In mid-July, word finally came. Billy was hiding out at Fort Sumner again. Garrett collected two deputies, Thomas McKinney and John Poe, and set off west.

The other residents of the dilapidated fort-town were either too sympathetic or too scared to give Garrett any details of the Kid's whereabouts. But then the lawman had a slice of luck that would change his life, and end that of Billy the Kid. Garrett knew that a reliable old acquaintance, Pedro or "Pete" Maxwell, was staying in

Fort Sumner, and paid him a midnight call to see if he had any information. On his way, Garrett saw a white man with some Mexicans in an orchard near outbuildings just sixty yards from Maxwell's house. The man was wearing shirtsleeves and a dark vest, but his sombrero and the darkness prevented Garrett from recognizing him.

## SHOWDOWN

Garrett and his two men crept toward Maxwell's house, and Garrett entered alone to find Pete in bed in a darkened room. Garrett sat on the bed, just by his friend's pillow, and asked him the whereabouts of the Kid. Garrett recalled: "At that moment a man sprang quickly into the door, looking back, and called twice in Spanish, 'Who comes there?'" The man was holding a revolver in one hand and a butcher's knife in the other. Garrett later learned that the man was the same white cowboy he had seen earlier, who had come

to Maxwell's house to slice off some beef for his supper. He must have caught sight of the deputies.

Garrett recounted: "He came directly towards me. Before he reached the bed, I whispered: 'Who is it, Pete?'" Fortunately, the room was so dark that the intruder could not initially see Garrett by the bed-head. Maxwell then told Garrett, "That's him!" The Kid spotted Garrett in the darkness and raised his pistol while retreating backward across the room.

Garrett acted fast. "Quickly as possible I drew my revolver and fired, threw my body aside, and fired again. The second shot was useless; the Kid fell dead. He never spoke. A struggle or two, a little strangling sound as he gasped for breath, and the Kid was with his many victims." The exact details of Garrett's testimony have been questioned, but by whatever means, he had killed Billy the Kid, the greatest young outlaw of the West. 🍂

# Jack the Ripper

## THE UNKNOWN SLASHER WHO BECAME THE MOST RENOWNED SERIAL KILLER OF ALL TIME

George Lusk of the Whitechapel Vigilance Committee opened a package and a fleshy object fell out. The sender's address given on the accompanying letter was simply "From hell," and the half-illiterate text read, "I send you half the Kidne I took from one women prasarved it for you tother piece I fried and it was very nise." The letter, opened on October 16, 1888, purported to be from the notorious killer known as Jack the Ripper, who had committed a series of gruesome murders in the London district of Whitechapel. The writer signed off with "Catch me if you can." Lusk never could catch him, and nor could anyone else. The identity of the most famous serial killer in history would remain a mystery for evermore.

Opposite:Jack the Ripper in one of his notorious slashing attacks, as depicted in the *Police Gazette*.

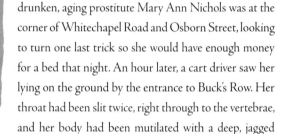

## ⤳ FACT FILE ↶

**Born:** Nineteenth century, probably United Kingdom.
**Died:** Unknown.
**Historic Feat:** Killed at least five women in Whitechapel, London, without detection.
**Circumstances of Death:** Unknown.
**Legacy:** The most famous unidentified serial killer in history.

Six weeks earlier, at 2:30 a.m. on August 31, 1888, the drunken, aging prostitute Mary Ann Nichols was at the corner of Whitechapel Road and Osborn Street, looking to turn one last trick so she would have enough money for a bed that night. An hour later, a cart driver saw her lying on the ground by the entrance to Buck's Row. Her throat had been slit twice, right through to the vertebrae, and her body had been mutilated with a deep, jagged wound in her lower abdomen and a series of cuts running left to right.

Nichols was the first victim in the five-person killing spree of Jack the Ripper. Other deaths in Whitechapel, both before and after the murders, would be linked to Jack, but those five followed a very particular modus operandi, involving both savagery and surgical care.

Whitechapel was a seedy, crime-riddled area frequented by more than 1,000 prostitutes. Murders

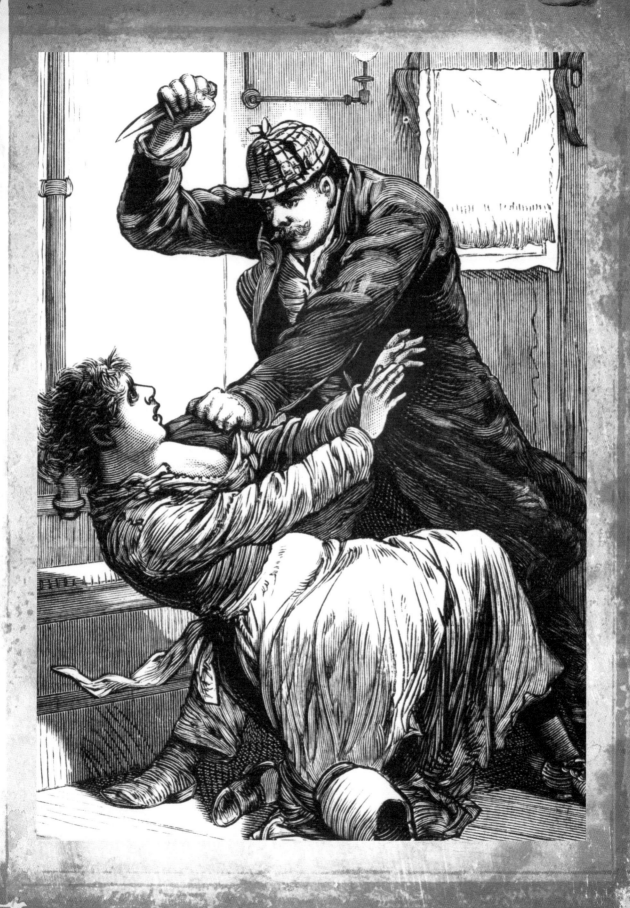

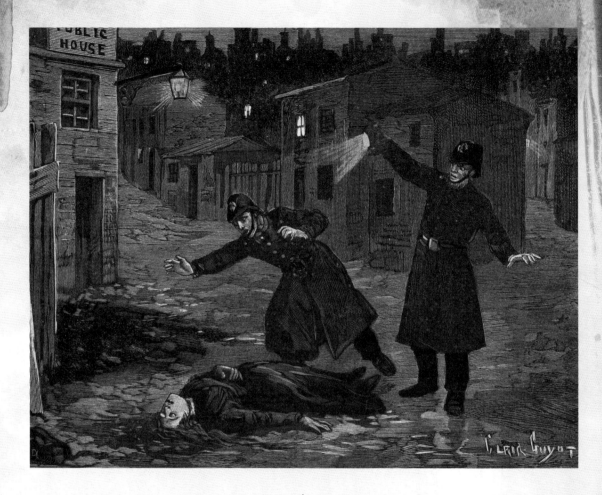

**Above:** Police discovering the body of one of Jack the Ripper's victims, as illustrated in *Le Petit Parisien*, 1891.
**Opposite:** The notorious "From hell" letter, purporting to be from the mysterious serial killer.

were commonplace, but a second murder, on September 8, made the local police inspector, Edmund Reid, fear that they had an especially vile killer on their hands. Annie Chapman had a similar profile to Nichols: aged 47, she had split from her husband and was working as a casual prostitute. At 5:30 a.m. she was seen talking to

a man with a dark complexion, a deerstalker hat, and a dark overcoat. Half an hour later, she was found dead in a nearby yard. Her throat had been severed deeply with a 6–8 inch (15–20 cm) knife; she had been disemboweled and part of her uterus had been cut out.

Next on the gruesome register was Elizabeth Stride, another Whitechapel prostitute in her 40s. Her body was discovered at 1 a.m. on September 30. A half hour earlier, a police constable had seen her outside a Jewish social club with a man wearing a hard felt hat and carrying a package. She was found with her throat slit by the club's steward while the blood was still running from the wound, but there was no abdominal mutilation. Another body was found hours later, supporting the theory that the Ripper had been disturbed in the act and had quickly found another victim to satisfy his depraved lust for ritual mutilation.

That victim was Catherine Eddowes, yet another casual prostitute with a taste for drink. She was seen talking to a man with a fair moustache and a peaked cloth cap at 1:35 a.m. Her mutilated, still-warm body was found just ten minutes later by a police constable. Her throat had been slit and she had been disemboweled. The police surgeon, Dr. Frederick Brown, noted a new twist to the ritual: "A piece [of intestine] of about two feet was quite detached from the body and placed between the body and the left arm, apparently by design." The left kidney had been removed, and Brown surmised: "It required a great deal of knowledge to have removed the kidney and to know where it was placed. Such a knowledge might be possessed by one in the habit of cutting up animals."

## CONTRADICTORY EVIDENCE

Reid's team had expanded to include Scotland Yard detectives but they remained mystified, as did the self-appointed Whitechapel Vigilance Committee. They were not aided by descriptions of the men seen talking to the women just prior to the murders. The Ripper seemed to be both dark and fair and have a vast assortment of clothing from shabby to well-dressed. He seemed likely to be a left-handed doctor, butcher, or tanner, while a wave of anti-Semitism in the area pointed the finger at the Jewish population. In fear of rioting, the police had to scrub away a chalked cryptic "confession"—"The Juwes are the men that will not be blamed for nothing"—found near Eddowes's bloodied apron. The authorities were also

being taunted by post, including with the "From Hell" letter, which was probably sent by a prankster. The police never came close to catching the killer, leading to dozens of different theories, not least that it was Prince Albert Victor, Queen Victoria's grandson.

A final murder followed on November 9, but the profile was somewhat different. Mary Jane Kelly was murdered in her own home and she was only 25 years old. Furthermore, the desecration of her body had been taken to a new extreme: her breasts had been cut off and her face slashed beyond recognition. There were no further murders that can safely be ascribed to the killer, so perhaps the Ripper had finally gorged his appetite to the point of satiation. Or, as some believe, he had gone to America to begin a new spree … ❧

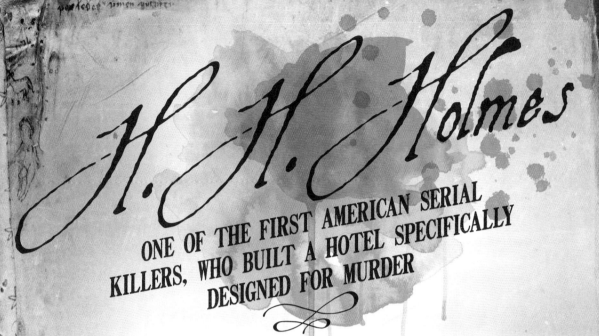

# H. H. Holmes

## ONE OF THE FIRST AMERICAN SERIAL KILLERS, WHO BUILT A HOTEL SPECIFICALLY DESIGNED FOR MURDER

The privileged little boy, Herman Webster Mudgett, was so scared of the doctor, illness, and death that his bullying classmates forced him to touch a human skeleton. Herman soon realized that what he feared was not the skeleton, but the extent of his own pleasure in its proximity. The episode unleashed a lifetime's obsession with death and he became a serial killer who ran his own "Murder Castle." Sometimes, he would gleefully strip a victim's cadaver down to the bone and sell the skeleton to medical schools. In his confession, written for a newspaper shortly before his execution, he referred to himself as "the most detestable criminal of modern times."

Mudgett was born in Gilmanton, New Hampshire, in 1861. Following

the incident at school, he took an interest in surgery and began to experiment on animals. As a medical student, already using the assumed name of Henry Howard Holmes, he would steal corpses and make false life insurance claims by faking accidents.

At the age of 25, he moved to Chicago and worked as an assistant in a pharmacy, which he soon bought from the owner. His plans expanded to a site across the road, where he built a three-story enterprise including a new pharmacy and other shops, living quarters, and hotel rooms. The peculiar building featured fake battlements and, in time, would be known as "Murder Castle." It would be revealed as the site of an extraordinary number of horrendous murders. Holmes would eventually confess to twenty-seven murders in total, but there are wilder estimates that he may have killed 200 people. Many of the victims who were lured

## FACT FILE

**Born:** May 16, 1861, Gilmanton.
**Died:** May 7, 1896, Philadelphia.
**Historic Feat:** Murdered at least twenty-seven and possibly as many as 200 people in his specially designed "Murder Castle."
**Circumstances of Death:** Hanged after being found guilty of murder.
**Legacy:** One of the earliest and most prolific serial killers in American history.

**Opposite:** Herman Webster Mudgett, better known as Dr. Henry Howard Holmes, in 1895.

148

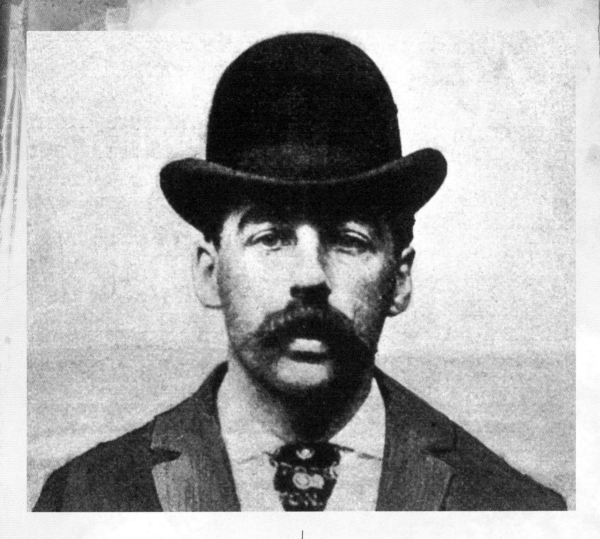

to the hotel were single women attending Chicago's World Fair of 1893, while others answered advertisements to work in Holmes's shops.

## PREYING ON THE VULNERABLE

A great number of the people who died at Murder Castle remain unknown, but the trail of up to fifty missing persons ended at its Englewood address. One of the known victims was Emeline Cigrand, a young stenographer from Dwight, Illinois, whom Holmes pursued after being told of her beauty by a criminal acquaintance, Benjamin Pitezel. Holmes lured her to the hotel with the promise of a job, locked her in a soundproof room and repeatedly raped her. He killed her, he later admitted, due to the jealousy of his wife, Minnie. When Emeline's fiancé, Robert Phelps, turned up looking for her, he was imprisoned and killed in what Holmes would later describe as a "stretching experiment."

Holmes was a bigamist and had several wives and mistresses, some of whose remains (including Minnie's) would be found in Murder Castle. However, it was an

33379
D.C. 9-2-28

## CARL PANZRAM

ANOTHER of the U.S.'s early serial killers who refused to show remorse was Carl Panzram, born in Minnesota in 1891: "In my lifetime I have murdered twenty-one human beings, I have committed thousands of burglaries, robberies, larcenies, arsons and, last but not least, I have committed sodomy on more than 1,000 male human beings. For all these things I am not in the least bit sorry." Panzram would often rape the men he robbed and killed, although he denied he was homosexual: he did it to show his dominance. At his execution, on September 5, 1930, he said, "Hurry it up, you Hoosier bastard. I could hang a dozen men while you're fooling around."

insurance scam—not murder—that led to Holmes's downfall.

In July 1894, Holmes was caught out using counterfeit notes and a false signature to buy some horses. While in custody, he told Marion Hedgepeth, a train robber, of his plan to swindle an insurance company by faking his own death. In exchange for a cut, Hedgepeth gave him details of a lawyer who could help the process. After Holmes's release on bail, he used a cadaver to fake his own death, but the plan failed because the insurance company refused to pay out. Undeterred, Holmes tried the trick again, this time with his accomplice Benjamin Pitezel as the "deceased." In the end, Holmes decided there was no need to fake the death, and killed Pitezel. He took the majority of the insurance payment from Pitezel's wife, having convinced her that her husband was just in hiding, but he planned to kill her later. In the meantime, Holmes took charge of three of her children.

Holmes had made the fatal mistake of not paying Hedgepeth for his information, and the crook went to the authorities. A Pinkerton agent called Frank P. Geyer tracked Holmes down and arrested him for the Pitezel insurance scam. He started to look more closely into Holmes's affairs and was mystified by the maze of lies, insurance frauds, and different identities that were associated with one single man. He was most perturbed by the unknown whereabouts of the three Pitezel children. He tracked Holmes's movements across the United States and Canada, and found the bodies of the

**Opposite:** H.H. Holmes's World's Fair Hotel, which became known as "Murder Castle" after it was revealed that up to 200 people were tortured and murdered within its walls.

two Pitezel girls in a house in Toronto. Holmes later confessed that he had tricked the children into hiding in a trunk and then gassed them. Then, in Indianapolis, Geyer found the charred remains of the third child.

## HOUSE OF MURDER

Geyer now requested to search Murder Castle. What he discovered was a macabre mansion designed for murder. The second floor was a labyrinth of passages and bizarre angles. Some of the rooms were windowless and soundproofed; some were lined with asbestos or sheet iron, with scorch marks on the walls; some had gas jets for gassing or burning. A small gas chamber included a chute so the victim's body could be sent straight down to the basement.

There, Geyer found a gruesome torture chamber featuring a dissecting table, surgical instruments, a rack, a vat of corrosive acid, and quicklime pits. There was also an incinerator. Bones from many different bodies were found along with items that revealed the fate of some of Holmes's wives and mistresses. The number of victims could not be determined from the mass of fragments.

Holmes, convicted as one of America's worst ever serial killers, later confessed to his crimes but he never repented. When he was hanged on May 7, 1896, it took him fifteen minutes to die, so perhaps he got a taste of what it must have been like for his countless victims. ✍

# Al Capone

## THE ULTIMATE AMERICAN GANGSTER WHO EVADED THE AUTHORITIES DESPITE BEING CONNECTED TO MULTIPLE MURDERS

In the mugshots from the early 1930s that adorn his criminal record sheet, Al Capone looks healthy, plump, and so self-assured that he is openly smiling. Despite being responsible for multiple homicides, he looks like a man who believes he will be released imminently due to some legal—or possibly illegal—sleight-of-hand.

The mugshots taken on July 1, 1939, after seven years of imprisonment, reveal a different man. The weight has gone after years of prison food and he does not seem to be in the best of health. The smile has gone, too, and so has the arrogance. In 1931, after the authorities had been trying to nail

**Opposite:** A cocky Al Capone winks at photographers as he leaves a Chicago courthouse on October 14, 1931, where he faced charges for income tax violations.

## ⟿ FACT FILE ⟿

**Born:** January 17, 1899, Brooklyn, New York.

**Died:** January 25, 1947, Palm Island, Florida.

**Historic Feat:** Head of the Chicago Outfit, a mob responsible for multiple murders.

**Circumstances of Death:** Cardiac arrest following a stroke and pneumonia.

**Legacy:** The most famous U.S. mobster, who made millions from the Prohibition era and evaded numerous murder charges.

the infamous mobster for years, they had finally got their man and made it stick. Capone had thought he was untouchable and had turned a whole district of Chicago into his personal gangland playground; when he emerged back into the light in November 1939, there would be no return to the glory days. The greatest American gangster ever known was finished.

Alphonse Gabriel Capone, the son of an Italian immigrant family, was born in Brooklyn, New York, on January 17, 1899. The violence and easy money of gang culture appealed to Capone from an early age and he left school after sixth grade to join Johnny Torrio's local street gang, which included future mob leader Charles "Lucky" Luciano in its numbers. Capone reputedly killed at least two men while working for the gang but, as

would remain the case throughout his career, he avoided prosecution for murder. Torrio moved to Chicago and became a lieutenant in the notorious Colosimo Mafia gang, and, in 1920 at the age of 21, Capone followed.

## IN CHICAGO

It was a step up from their Brooklyn activities. The Colosimo mob was effectively a huge armed business, running more than 200 brothels as well as an extortion racket. The gang also developed more legitimate businesses in the textile industry, and through the use of blackmail, bribes, and favors, exerted influence over

**Below:** Police photographs of Capone immediately after his arrest in 1931.
**Opposite:** Crowds gather outside a garage at 2122 North Clark Street, Chicago, and witness the body of a victim of the St. Valentine's Day Massacre being removed.

the labor unions and public officials. Torrio wanted the gang to take full advantage of the possibilities for illegal trade brought about by the Eighteenth Amendment, which prohibited the production, sale, and transport of alcohol from January 1920. The boss, "Big" Jim Colosimo, refused—and was shot and killed in May. While Torrio was never prosecuted, it seems certain that he arranged the hit, with either Capone or Frankie Yale, another of his former New York colleagues, pulling the trigger. Capone, whose reputation for violence was growing, was arrested in 1924 for a separate murder, but released.

Torrio took over the mob, which was rechristened "the Chicago Outfit," and extended its enterprises until 1925, when he was mown down by the rival North Side gang in a hail of gunfire. He survived, but had been hit multiple times and handed his empire over to his favorite henchman. Capone would prove to be a clever and utterly ruthless gang boss who set out to annihilate rival gangs in Chicago and

C28169

turned the suburb of Cicero into his own lawless domain. He was charged for a triple homicide in 1926, and repeatedly arrested for other major offences, but the authorities could not make any of the charges stick. Meanwhile, his enterprise was allegedly worth more than $100 million per annum through prostitution, gambling, extortion, and, primarily, the illegal sale of alcohol.

## ST. VALENTINE'S DAY MASSACRE

On February 14, 1929, gangland violence reached a new level. George "Bugs" Moran's North Side mob had repeatedly stepped on the toes of the Chicago Outfit through a number of successful and failed assassinations, and Capone allegedly sought to end the dispute once and for all. Seven North Side gangsters were caught in a liquor warehouse by mobsters dressed as policemen, lined up against a wall and machine-gunned down. Capone would never be charged for the murders because he could prove that he was staying at his estate in Florida at the time.

Meanwhile, the Bureau of Investigation (the future FBI) and the U.S. Treasury Department were taking an interest in Capone's illegal alcohol business and financial affairs, since there seemed little chance that he would ever be successfully prosecuted for murder. However,

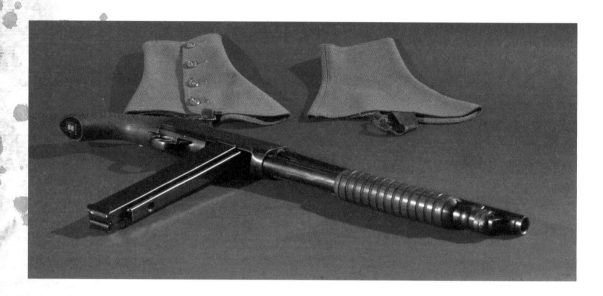

## MURDER INC.

UNLIKE Al Capone, the American mobster Louis Buchalter did not manage to evade the electric chair. Buchalter ran a racketeering enterprise in the garment district of New York in the 1920s and was arrested for the murder of a bootlegger in 1927. The charges were dropped and Buchalter took his criminal career to another level. In the 1930s, he formed a criminal organization later nicknamed Murder, Inc., offering assassination services to Cosa Nostra mobsters. By 1935, Buchalter had 250 operatives and drugs smugglers working for him. Following a huge FBI manhunt, Buchalter gave himself up in 1939. He was sent to the electric chair for just four of the dozens of murders he had authorized.

the authorities did meet with some success later in 1929 when Capone was arrested in Philadelphia and charged with possession of a concealed weapon. He was sentenced to one year and released after nine months, for good behavior, on March 17, 1930, but was tried again in 1931 for contempt of court. During that time, Bureau and Treasury resources focused even more intently on prosecuting Capone for income tax evasion.

## PURSUED BY THE TAXMAN

Agents amassed evidence that Capone owed $215,000 in taxes from his gambling profits, and in June 1931 he was brought to court, facing additional charges of failing to file tax returns and violating Prohibition laws. Capone was not unduly worried. He pled guilty, telling the press that he would arrange a plea bargain and only be given a sentence of two-and-a-half years. Judge James H. Wilkerson had other ideas, so Capone changed his plea to not guilty. Capone was still not worried—he simply bribed the jury. Then, in a masterstroke, Wilkerson switched the jury at the last minute. Capone was sentenced to eleven years, along with a concurrent six-month sentence for the contempt-of-court charge, as well as having to pay his back taxes and a fine of $50,000. He had sidestepped justice for multiple murders, but the taxman had got him. The smile was finally wiped off Capone's face.

He served seven-and-a-half years, several of which were spent in virtual isolation in the new high-security prison on Alcatraz Island in San Francisco Bay; he was cut off from his fellow gang members and his power and influence ebbed away. During his imprisonment his health also declined, and he started to show signs of dementia related to syphilis, the venereal disease. On his release in 1939, he was unable to retake the throne as the King of the Chicago Mob. Instead, he was immediately transferred to a hospital to have treatment. He retired to his estate on Palm Island near Miami in Florida, and the dementia slowly took greater hold. By 1946, a psychiatrist assessed the once mentally agile gangland

boss as having the mental age of a 12-year-old boy. Soon afterward, on January 25, 1947, he passed away, having suffered a stroke and pneumonia.

Meanwhile, the Prohibition era had ended in 1933 with the repeal of the Eighteenth Amendment. The policy had succeeded in cutting alcohol consumption in the United States by half but had opened the door to a huge rise in illegal gangland activity, augmented by a steep increase in inter-gang killings as the financial rewards were so great. No mob boss would ever again have the notoriety of Al Capone, even when the gangs took up drug trafficking as their deadly but profitable enterprise. ❧

**Below:** Cells at Alcatraz Federal Penitentiary, where Al Capone was incarcerated from 1934 to 1939.
**Opposite:** Gun and spats used by the American gangster Al Capone, otherwise known as Scarface.

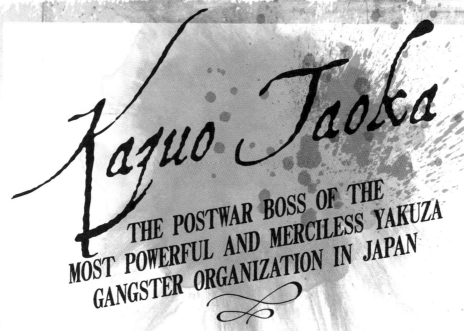

# Kazuo Taoka

## THE POSTWAR BOSS OF THE MOST POWERFUL AND MERCILESS YAKUZA GANGSTER ORGANIZATION IN JAPAN

The mysterious tattooed yakuza, the Japanese organized crime members, may be ruthless in dealing with each other and their enemies, but many have a strong code of conduct and even draw some level of inspiration from the samurai "way of the warrior." Yakuza even refer to themselves as *ninkyō dantai* ("chivalrous organizations"), although the police prefer the less graceful term *bōryokudan* ("violence group"). In the 1930s, the yakuza godfather—or *oyabun*—Yoshio Kodama started to take organized criminality and political interference to new levels, but he still held street-level savagery in high disdain and regarded himself as a man of honor.

The same could not be said of Kazuo Taoka, a brawler who became

**Opposite:** From left to right, Ono Mitsuru, Taoka Kazuo, and Tsuruta Koji. Koji was an actor who famously starred in a number of 1960s films as a chivalric but world-weary yakuza.

the most important yakuza figure in history. He and his gang members were permanently drenched in other people's blood and left a trail of corpses from street level right up to the penthouse.

## A SELF-MADE MAN

An orphan born in 1912, Taoka literally carved out his future on the streets and docks of Kobe. He was deft with a blade, but most famous for clawing at the eyes of his opponents, leading to his nickname of Kuma, "The Bear." Working for the Yamaguchi-gumi, a yakuza family, he organized cheap labor to sell in the dockyards until he was imprisoned for six years for the murder of a gang rival in 1937.

He returned to the Yamaguchi-gumi fold on his release and took charge three years later, although at the time the outfit had only a couple of dozen gang members. Taoka's rare

> ### ~ FACT FILE ~
>
> **Born:** March 28, 1913, Higashimiyoshi.
> **Died:** July 23, 1981, Amagasaki.
> **Historic Feat:** Brought a new level of organized crime and violence to the streets of Japan.
> **Circumstances of death:** Heart attack.
> **Legacy:** Yakuza became more prevalent in Japan, leading to anti-gang laws.

mix of organizational genius and an exceptionally violent nature proved to be gold dust in the chaos of postwar Japan. During his thirty-five years as godfather, the Yamaguchi-gumi ranks swelled to contain over 10,000 soldiers based all over Japan and the clan ran 2,500 businesses as well as huge loan-shark, gambling, prostitution, extortion, and smuggling operations. He also expanded his interests into the field of sport and entertainment. Taoka did not just run the biggest organized-crime syndicate in Japan: he effectively ran one of the country's biggest businesses.

After taking control of the Yamaguchi-gumi, Taoka made a pact with the largest gambling gang in Kobe, but he was not a man to enjoy ruling by committee so his soldiers blew away the old-style gangsters and took over their operations. He then spread his interests to the city of Osaka, where the dominant Korean gang suffered the same fate. Its members either complied with Taoka's demands for a cut or

gangland executions would follow. Next in his systematic campaign for Nippon-domination were the yakuza of other large cities, and he subsumed their soldiers—at least, the ones that lived—into his own organization.

By the 1960s, even Kodama was scared; he was so wary that the Yamaguchi-gumi would step into his home patch of Yokohama that he was forced to negotiate terms with Taoka. However, the authorities had also taken note of Taoka's involvement in the tsunami of violence and criminality: the National Police Agency began to monitor his activities closely in 1963. Three years later, he was indicted on five counts, which included blackmail, but the police could not charge the yakuza godfather for murder despite the high body count and the vast size of his illegal operations. Even pinning Taoka down on the lesser counts would prove to be a decades-long process because he was protected by excellent legal teams and well versed in the art of bribery.

## YAKUZA

**YAKUZA** emerged in seventeenth-century Japan and originally ran illegal gambling operations or peddled stolen goods, but later added more violent crimes to their roster. Despite their criminality, they developed a series of traditions and a strict code of honor. A soldier is a *kobun* ("foster-child") who swears allegiance to the *oyabun* ("foster-father") by drinking from the same cup of saké. If a soldier does anything wrong, he cuts off the end of his little finger and gives it to the oyabun by way of apology. More sections of fingers follow on further offenses. Yakuza have full-body tattoos, but not on their face or hands so they can keep them hidden.

## GANGSTER PACT

In 1972 Kodama, ever the gentleman if such could be found in the ranks of gangsters, negotiated a pact between the Yamaguchi-gumi and the Inagawa-gai, the main yakuza gang in Tokyo, in order to prevent more bloodshed in inter-gang warfare. The sides met at Taoka's own residence and conducted a traditional *sakazuki* ceremony, swearing their allegiance before drinking saké from ceremonial cups. The result was a colossal yakuza organization.

The authorities still could not get close to Taoka, but a young man called Kiyoshi Narumi could. Taoka's men had killed the godfather of the Matsuda gang, which operated in western Japan, and Narumi, a young gang member, had symbolically eaten his cremated *oyabun*'s ashes and vowed revenge. In 1978, while Taoka was watching a limbo-dancing performance at a nightclub in Kyoto, Narumi managed to avoid the cohort of Yamaguchi-gumi bodyguards for long enough to shoot Taoka in the neck and escape. Taoka survived the assassination attempt; Narumi was not so fortunate. His corpse turned up a couple of weeks later in a remote spot outside Kobe. We can assume that his death had not been a swift and painless process.

The prosecution of charges against Taoka came to a head in 1981, with the Kobe district court finally ready to sentence him that summer. However, by then Taoka was already dead, having had a heart attack on July 23. Despite anti-gang laws, the Japanese authorities have still not managed effectively to rein in the activities of the yakuza. There are now over 100,000 yakuza—more than half of whom are members of the Yamaguchi-gumi—and their influence has spread throughout eastern Asia, Hawaii, and the west coast of the United States of America. ◗

**Opposite:** A gang member gets another tattoo, 1946.

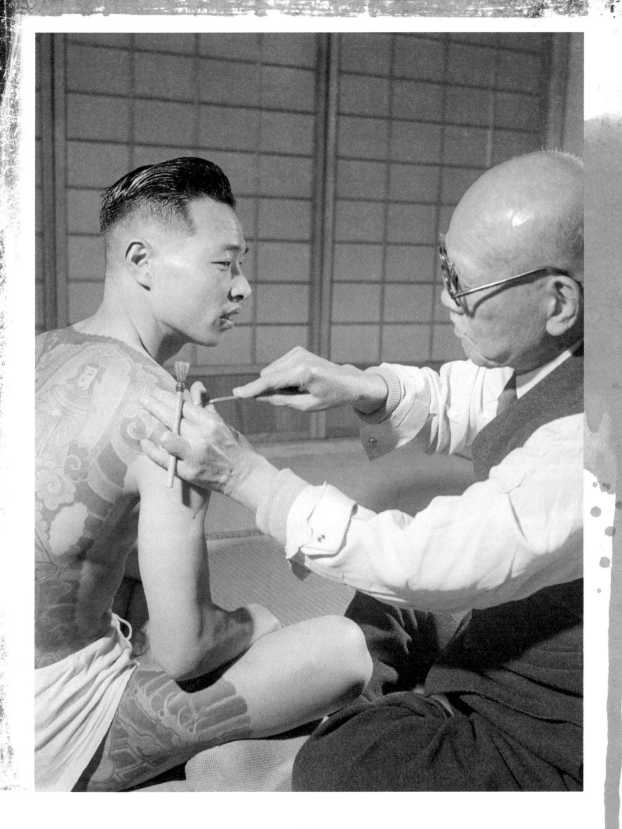

# Joseph Stalin

## THE SOVIET LEADER WHO RUTHLESSLY ELIMINATED HIS ENEMIES

Joseph Stalin was simultaneously one of the greatest and worst leaders known to history. He helped to save Europe from Nazi domination and, under his leadership, the huge nation of Russia began to achieve its great potential as a world superpower. However, this came at the cost of millions of lives as he mercilessly eradicated all opposition, annexed countries, and put in place policies that resulted in mass poverty and starvation. He undertook a combination of political and ethnic genocide on a massive scale while suffering from a deep-seated paranoia. Away from the battlefield, he was personally responsible for more deaths than Nazi leader Adolf Hitler. Despite this, he was loved by many Russians, even after his

**Opposite:** Joseph Stalin and a group of Central Committee members in Red Square, Moscow, 1945.

cruelty was exposed following his death.

Like Hitler, Stalin was not born within the borders of the country he would lead. He was born Iosif Vissarionovich Dzhugashvili in Georgia, part of the Russian Empire, in 1879. He trained to become a priest, but he was expelled from the seminary. He would later dominate the Soviet Union through the cult of personality—a policy of deliberate myth-making about his personal greatness: according to the official version of his past, he was expelled for distributing Marxist propaganda, but in fact it was for missing some tests.

### "MAN OF STEEL"

He would also claim to have played an essential role in the rise of communism in Russia. He joined Lenin's Bolshevik Communist Party in 1903, and actively opposed tsarist rule of the empire. Around 1912 he adopted the name "Stalin,"

### FACT FILE

**Born:** December 21, 1879, Gori.

**Died:** March 5, 1953, Kuntsevo.

**Historic Feat:** Turned the Soviet Union into a major industrialized nation and a superpower.

**Circumstances of Death:** Stroke.

**Legacy:** Still a hero to some Russians, he was responsible for more than 20 million deaths through economic policies, deportations, and executions.

which means "man of steel" and hinted at his future mercilessness. Despite being temporarily expelled to Siberia for his activities, he was far from being a major player in the revolutions of 1917, which brought the Bolsheviks to power.

He became a member of Lenin's cabinet and his strength of personality attracted enough of a following for him to become general secretary of the Communist Party in 1922

**Below:** Stalin with his daughter Svetlana, 1935.
**Opposite:** 27 million Soviet lives were lost in the Second World War, but the outcome enabled Stalin to dominate Eastern Europe in the postwar period.

and one of the major figures vying for control with Leon Trotsky after Lenin died in 1924. Trotsky was opposed to Stalin's desire to create "socialism in one country," but Stalin orchestrated his removal from the Communist Party, and then the country. Finally, even though Trotsky became a marginal, politically impotent figure living in Mexico, Stalin had him assassinated in 1940. In the meantime, Stalin became the effective dictator of the empire, which had been christened the Soviet Union in 1922.

## COLLECTIVIZATION

An integral part of Stalin's economic policy was the state collectivization of all industry and agriculture in the Soviet Union from 1928 onward. Industry began to

thrive, but his system of five-year plans created almost impossible productivity targets for workers, who were paid a pittance and faced extreme rationing, while rapid centralization destroyed agricultural productivity. The *kulaks*, the broad class of farmers, were stripped of all their property and wealth, and executed or deported to work in labor camps. The result of collectivization was the devastating famine of 1932–33, in which 6 million people died.

Stalin was paranoid about opposition to the inhumanity of his restructuring of the Soviet Union, and set about the Great Purge of 1936–38, in which 250,000 people were killed as "enemies of the people." The remaining members of Lenin's cabinet and a huge number of army officers were executed on the basis of concocted evidence. Over the course of Stalin's rule, 14 million people were enslaved in the gulag system of labor camps. The conditions in the gulags, some of the largest of which were in Siberia with winter temperatures falling as low as -49°F (-45°C), were unendurable for many: 1.7 million people died. During the 1940s, 1 million members of ethnic minorities, allegedly rebellious against the true Soviet ideal, were displaced by Stalin's key henchman, Lavrentiy Beria, and faced starvation on desolate land.

Due to the personality cult, the image of the leader was increasingly at odds with the monstrous reality of the man. He was portrayed as the savior of the Soviet

## STALIN'S VICTIMS

ESTIMATES of the number of people who died as a result of the actions of Joseph Stalin, Soviet leader from c. 1924 to 1953, vary greatly, but even conservative estimates place the figure at 20 million. Around 250,000 people died in the Great Purge, when Stalin sought to wipe out all opposition. The total death toll includes individual political assassinations, but many deaths were the result of his devastating agricultural policies (6 million in the 1932–33 famine alone), the Gulag labor camps (1.7 million), and the enforced deportation of people to remote, uncultivated areas (more than 1 million).

people and was granted titles such as the "Brilliant Genius of Humanity," while statues of him were put up in towns across the Union.

In the Second World War, Stalin initially made a pact with Hitler so that he could reclaim former territories of the Russian empire without opposition. However, in 1941, the two leaders began a monumental fight for control of eastern Europe. Stalin's indifference to the value of human life came to the fore on a grand scale: 27 million Soviet lives were taken on the eastern front.

Soviet control of the east gave Stalin pole position in the chaos at the cessation of war. East Germany

**Above:** Two girls dressed in warm clothes in Ust-Omtschug, a Siberian town which was the center of Stalin's Gulag system in the Magadan region.
**Opposite:** Russian President Dmitry Medvedev lays flowers at the Mask of Sorrow monument in Magadan, which commemorates the millions of victims of Gulag labor camps.

and most of eastern Europe effectively became Soviet satellite countries, and Stalin was now master of a world superpower that rivaled the United States.

The Cold War, with Western democracies ranged against the "Eastern Bloc" of Stalin's communist/autocratic hybrid countries, began, as did the persecution of opposition in the new bloc behind the "Iron Curtain."

Stalin's campaigns against his perceived enemies—political, personal, ethnic, or religious—continued until his death from a stroke on March 5, 1953. His successor, Nikita Khrushchev, formally denounced his personality cult in 1956, but Russia and Eastern Europe would not be free of the shackles of Stalin-style communism and police-state culture for decades to come.

# Lee Harvey Oswald

## THE YOUNG GUNMAN WHO ASSASSINATED U.S. PRESIDENT JOHN F. KENNEDY

**N**o one paid much attention to the new boy sitting in the seventh grade class in the Bronx. There was nothing special about him: he was neither the brightest nor the worst in the class and, to begin with, he caused the teachers no real concern. And yet, just a dozen years later, Lee Harvey Oswald would decide to slay the golden boy of U.S. politics: John F. Kennedy, president of the United States. Mayhem and wild national grief ensued, and two days later Oswald, too, would be assassinated in a set of circumstances that remain imbued with mystery.

Perhaps the fact that no one paid much attention to Lee Harvey Oswald as a child fueled his journey to become the world's most notorious assassin. Two months before Oswald was born in New Orleans, Louisiana, on October 18, 1939, his father died of a heart attack. His mother, Marguerite, could not cope with Lee and his two

older brothers, and he spent some time in an orphanage. The family left for a fresh start in Texas, but ended up in the Bronx, New York, in 1952. It was a tough life in a tough neighborhood, with the single mother working long shifts to make ends meet. The youngest boy was often neglected and, by the age of 13, the rot had set in: Oswald was regularly playing truant and getting into trouble on the streets. A psychiatric assessment in a juvenile reformatory revealed that the boy was a "disturbed youngster who suffers under the impact of really existing emotional isolation and deprivation, lack of affection, absence of family life and rejection by a self involved and conflicted mother." He acted like "a kid nobody gave a darn about," and he did not give a darn about anyone else in return.

Oswald and Marguerite returned to New Orleans, then moved to Fort Worth, Texas,

## FACT FILE

**Born:** October 18, 1939, New Orleans.

**Died:** November 24, 1963, Dallas.

**Historic Feat:** Assassinated the president of the United States.

**Circumstances of Death:** Assassinated by Jack Ruby.

**Legacy:** The most notorious assassin in history, whose life and death remain the subject of conspiracy theories.

and at age 17 he joined the U.S. Marines. He had skills—somewhat chillingly, with hindsight, he proved to be a creditable marksman and was designated a "sharpshooter"—but he was still refusing to toe the line as far as authority was concerned. He was court-martialed twice in 1958 for having an illegal weapon and violent behavior. By this time, he was already a loaded gun that sooner or later would explode into life.

Having read socialist literature as a boy, he felt that the U.S., capitalism, and democracy had let him down. The malcontent left the Marines and in October 1959 went to live in the Soviet Union, where he was not welcomed with open arms: he was forced to undergo psychiatric assessment and was kept under surveillance. He married Marina Prusakova and had a daughter, but his unhappiness soon resurfaced again. In June 1962 he returned to the States with his family to live in Texas, but he remained enthralled by Marxism. He supported communist Cuba, which the CIA, with the blessing of Kennedy, had attempted to destabilize in an abortive

**Above:** Lee Harvey Oswald standing outside his home holding the weapon he used to kill John F. Kennedy.

invasion at the Bay of Pigs in 1961.

Oswald was quietly readying himself for action, and purchased a .38 handgun and a Carcano rifle. His trial run for the murder of the president came on April 10, 1963, when he attempted to assassinate Edwin A. Walker, an ex-U.S. major known for his anti-communist views, through the window of his home. Walker only suffered minor injuries to his arm.

Oswald then spent time in Mexico while failing to gain entry into Cuba. By October 16, he was back in Texas, working at the School Book Depository in Dallas. There, an opportunity to vent his anger at the United States fell right at his feet. John F. Kennedy, for many

**Above:** Dealey Plaza, Dallas, Texas: the location of the assassination of President Kennedy.
**Opposite:** President Kennedy seated next to his wife Jacqueline, and behind Governor Connally, just minutes before his assassination on November 22, 1963.

people the champion of the free world, was due to visit Dallas on November 22, 1963, and his motorcade would pass the book depository.

## SHOTS THAT SHOCKED THE WORLD

At 12:30 p.m. Kennedy and his wife Jackie, sitting in an open-topped limousine, swept slowly through Dealey Plaza while massed crowds filled the pavements to catch a glimpse of their charismatic idol. By then, Lee Harvey Oswald was already in position on the sixth floor of the depository, rifle at the ready. Three shots rang out. The first missed the vehicle. The second hit Kennedy in the upper shoulder and passed through him to wound the Governor of Texas, John B. Connally. The final shot hit Kennedy in the back of the head. Blood, brains, and bone fragments peppered the interior of the limousine.

The vehicle was driven straight to Parkland Memorial Hospital, with Jackie reportedly saying, "They have killed my husband and I have his brains in my hand." At 1 p.m.

Kennedy was pronounced dead. Meanwhile, a man sitting across the street from the depository had given a description of the gunman to the police.

Oswald was not done with the bloodshed. After the shooting he remained calm and was seen acting normal, carrying a Coke, on the second floor of the Book Depository. Before the building could be sealed off, he went home and changed his jacket. At 1:15 p.m. Police Officer J.D. Tippit saw Oswald walking down a street and stopped him, no doubt having been alerted to the description of the sniper. Oswald killed him with

**Above:** Lee Harvey Oswald following his arrest.
**Opposite:** The assassin received a cut to his forehead and a black eye while being apprehended at the Texas Theater.

four shots from his revolver. The assassin tried to hide out at the Texas Theater and was apprehended after he attempted to shoot another officer.

Meanwhile, the world went into shock. Famously, the question, "Where were you when Kennedy was shot?" could be answered by millions for decades to come. To many, the charming young president, who pushed forward civil rights and liberal policies, was the man of the future. But within a second his potential had been snuffed out.

## THE ASSASSIN ASSASSINATED

Oswald was interrogated for two days and denied both murders. The evidence was stacked against him but he would never face trial. On November 24, 1963, Oswald was being moved under armed escort from the police headquarters to the county jail when a stocky, suited figure stepped out of the crowd and fired a shot into his body. Oswald was taken to the same hospital as Kennedy and pronounced dead, so the world would never learn the full details of his motivations.

His killer was Jack Ruby, a nightclub owner who claimed he was acting in revenge, but he was known to have mob connections and Mafia-linked conspiracy theories still roll on to this day. Further questions over the whole affair have repeatedly arisen, with doubts over Oswald's ability to fire three bullets in such rapid succession and supposed irregularities about the location of the gunshot noises, raising suspicions that there was more than one gunman. Whatever the truth, Oswald, the unhappy boy who had been trained to kill and spent his adult life looking for a cause, had found his target and shocked the world. ✐

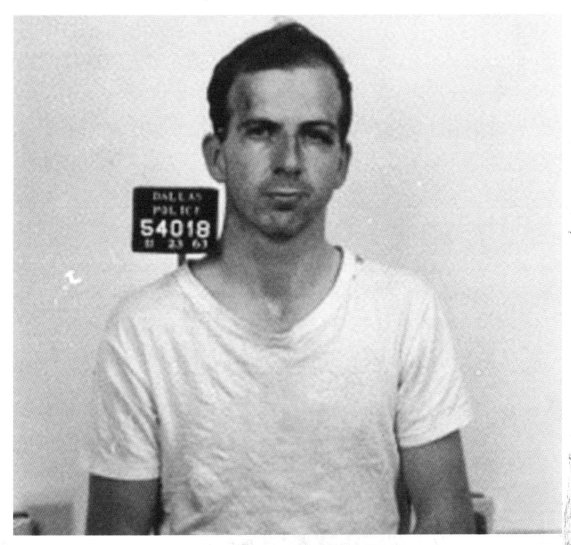

# Index

Page numbers in **bold** refer to illustrations.

## *Acknowledgments*

Quantum Books would like to thank the following agencies for supplying images for inclusion in this book:

Page 7, Chris Heller/Corbis; page 8 both, Wikipedia; page 9, Chris Hellier/Alamy; page 13, De Agostini/L. Romano/Getty Images; page 14, Montagu Images/Alamy; page 17, Mary Evans Picture Library/Alamy; page 18, Wikipedia; page 19, Wikipedia; page 20, Wikipedia; page 21, Mary Evans Picture Library/Alamy; page 23, Leemage/Getty Images; page 24, Wikipedia; page 25, Jonny Jim/iStock; page 27, Stefano Bianchetti/Corbis; page 28, Tarker/Corbis; page 29, Wikipedia; page 30, Heritage Images/Getty Images; page 31, Emi Cristea/Shutterstock.com; page 33, Wikipedia; page 34, Wikipedia; page 35, Print Collector/Contributor/Getty Images; page 36, Marek Stefunko/Shutterstock.com; page 37, Georgios Kollidas/Shutterstock.com; page 39, Heritage Images/Corbis; page 40, Print Collector/Getty Images; page 41, Wellcome Library, London; page 42, Wikipedia; page 43 top, Bettmann/corbis; page 43 bottom, Mary Evans Picture Library; page 45, Ivy Close Images/Alamy; page 46, Interim Archives/Getty Images; page 47, Wikipedia; page 49, Mary Evans Picture Library/Alamy; page 51, Wikipedia; page 52, Wikipedia; page 53, Universal Images Group/Getty; page 55, Keystone-France/Getty; page 56, Heritage Image Partnership Ltd./Alamy; page 57, Wikipedia; page 59, ITAR-TASS Photo Agency/Alamy; page 60, Wikipedia; page 61, Wikipedia; page 62 all, Wikipedia; page 67, Wikipedia; page 68, Wellcome Library, London; page 69, DEA PICTURE LIBRARY/Getty Images; page 71, Wellcome Library, London; page 72, Lagui/Shutterstock.com; page 73, Wellcome Library, London; page 75, Javier Espuny/Shutterstock.com; page 77, Renata Sedmakova Shutterstock.com; page 78, Wellcome Library, London; page 79, Leemage/Corbis; page 80, Debra Law/Shutterstock.com; page 81, Leemage/Corbis; page 83, Wellcome Library, London; page 84, Popperfoto/Getty Images; page 85, Wellcome Library, London; page 87, Wikipedia; page 88, Wellcome Library, London; page 89, Culture Club/Getty; page 91, Wikipedia; page 92, Wikipedia; page 93, Wikipedia; page 95, GL Archive/Alamy; page 96, Wikipedia; page 97, Hulton-Deutsch Collection/Corbis; page 98, Sovfoto/Getty Images; page 99, INTERFOTO/Alamy; page 101, Wikipedia; page 102; Wikipedia; page 103, Hulton-Deutsch Collection/Corbis; Page 104, Hulton-Deutsch Collection/Corbis; page 105, Hulton-Deutsch Collection/Corbis; page 107, Hulton-Deutsch Collection/Corbis; page 108, Bettmann/Corbis; page 109 top, Wikpedia; page 109 bottom, Bettmann/Corbis; page 111, Wikipedia; page 112, Wikipedia; page 113, Hulton-Deutsch Collection/Corbis; page 114, Bettmann/Corbis; page 115 both, Wikipedia; page 117, Orjan F. Ellingvag/Dagens Naringsliv/Corbis; page 118, Corbis; page 119, Corbis; page 123, Wikipedia; page 124, SuperStock/Getty; page 125, American School/Getty; page 127, Stapleton Collection/Corbis; page 128, English School/Getty; page 129, Wikipedia; page 131, Wellcome Library, London; page 132, Wikipedia; page 133, Wikipedia; page 135, Bettmann/Corbis; page 137 right, Wikipedia; page 137 left, Neveshkin Nikolay/Shutterstock.com; page 139, GL Archive/Alamy; page 140, Wikipedia; page 141, Everett Collection Historical/Alamy; page 142 left, Danita Delimont/Alamy; page 142 right, Wikipedia; page 143, Getty Images; page 145, Bettmann/Corbis; page 146, Leemage/Corbis; page 147, Wikipedia; page 149, Wikipedia; page 150, Bettmann/Corbis; page 151, Chicago History Museum/Getty; page 153, Bettmann/Corbis; page 154, Bettmann/Corbis; page 155, Chicago History Museum/Contributor; page 156, Hulton Archive/Staff; page 157, Jeff Whyte/Shutterstock.com; page 159, Wikipedia; page 160, Wikipedia; page 161, Horace Bristol/Corbis; page 163, Pictorial Press Ltd./Alamy; page 164, Wikipedia; page 165, dpa/dpa/Corbis; page 166, Barry Lewis/In Pictures/Corbis; page 167, Dmitry Astakhov/Pool/epa/Corbis; page 169, Donald Uhrbrock/Contributor; page 170, William A. Mueller/Shutterstock.com; page 171, Pictorial Press Ltd./Alamy; page 172, Bettmann/Corbis; page 173, Mug Shot/Alamy.

Every effort has been made to contact the copyright holders for images reproduced in this book. The publishers would welcome any errors or omissions being brought to their attention.